CW01509469

Shadows Merely Indicate

Shadows Merely Indicate

MICHAEL NILSEN

Copyright © 2020 Michael Nilsen

The moral right of the author has been asserted.

Apart from any fair dealing for the purposes of research or private study,
or criticism or review, as permitted under the Copyright, Designs and Patents
Act 1988, this publication may only be reproduced, stored or transmitted, in
any form or by any means, with the prior permission in writing of the
publishers, or in the case of reprographic reproduction in accordance with
the terms of licences issued by the Copyright Licensing Agency. Enquiries
concerning reproduction outside those terms should be sent to the publishers.

Matador
9 Priory Business Park,
Wistow Road, Kibworth Beauchamp,
Leicestershire. LE8 0RX
Tel: 0116 279 2299
Email: books@troubador.co.uk
Web: www.troubador.co.uk/matador
Twitter: @matadorbooks

ISBN 978 1838592 912

British Library Cataloguing in Publication Data.
A catalogue record for this book is available from the British Library.

Printed and bound in the UK by TJ International, Padstow, Cornwall
Typeset in 11pt Aldine401 BT by Troubador Publishing Ltd, Leicester, UK

Matador is an imprint of Troubador Publishing Ltd

To my nieces, nephew and great nephew:
Holly, Amy, Lauren, Jason and Theo.
You are all great people and may you always
find happiness in your lives.

I hadn't slept the night before. Stoned all night with my mate. Great preparation for uni! So when I got there, Luton, just outside London, I was wondering what I was letting myself in for. Aeroplanes roared overhead adding to the sense of excitement. The Muslims in there niqabs, eyes ablaze glaring at this wide eyed Grimberian. I wouldn't want to see all women dressed like that! Black people, Asians, White people, filed by. I spoke with a Northern accent, the first time I was aware I had one. Southerners raised their eye brows. The place buzzed, a community hub. How I reveled in the change of ambience. I soon ascertained how to score weed. Weed! Luton was the ganja capital. The record shops played Jamaican reggae. My house mate introduced me to Oasis. Whenever I hear *Wonderwall* I recall my first days in Luton. Down our street we were one of the few whites. I dug it. It was novel for a while. It was like living in India or Pakistan. I always wanted to visit the Indian ancient temples. And in my final year, to cut a long story short, I ardently fell in love with an Indian girl, unrequited I may add. Rupa was her name. At first I thought she said her name was Roofer! I asked her, what is the main principle of Hinduism? 'Live and let live,' she replied. Yes, live and let live, beautiful.

20-2-18

I am crow.
Hatched in human home.
Cramped cage.
Steel bars hem wings.
Sky filled feathers
Slide through window.
Blood glides
On stormy clouds.
Domesticated,
But ancient woodland
Croaks.

9-3-18

In a minute
You have
A million expressions.
Each twinkle
Of your eye
A valuable lesson.
Whatever you say
Has me
Transfixed.
The time
With you
Passes so quick.

15-3-18

We are people of the sun.
We were born to laugh and run.
Our skin is ancient stardust.
Galaxies swirl in our eyes.

I see the ice gradually thaw
As words tumble from your mouth.
I see you unfold before me
After all the years of drought.

22-3-18

The shimmering sea is heaving.
Foaming waves are breathing.
To the shore oceanic patterns weaving.

The breakers defiantly roar,
As Viking seas of yore,
Whispering ancient mariner lore.

Everyone mesmerically drawn to the sea.
The salty air we reverently breathe.
The coastline offers welcome reprieve.

23-3-18

The problem with having something valuable,
You can always be anxious about losing it.
Buddhism teaches us not to develop attachments,
As everything is transient.
There was life before my gold plated pen;
Life during my gold plated pen;
And now life after my gold plated pen.
I write this with a stainless steel Parker pen,
Not so grand as a gold plated pen.
My grandad gave me the gold plated pen before he died.
Of course, he could not have given me it after he died,
Unless bequeathed me in a will.
I'm just letting you know he died,
Which increases the sentimentality value.
I took the gold plated pen with me where ever I went to live:
Luton, Norwich, Walsall.
I must have kept the gold plated pen safe,
Though never used it.
But around 10 years ago
I started writing with the gold plated pen.
I grew rather attached to it.
Even wrote a poem about Mother Nature
Magically bestowing upon me a gold pen
So I could write poetry about ancient woodlands.
I took a photo of my hand holding the gold plated pen,
And posted it on Facebook
Explaining the significance of it.
And now, the gold plated pen has vanished…

I searched over and over again.
I looked in all the likely places,
And some unlikely too.
Was it Einstein who said: 'The definition of madness
Is doing the same thing over and over again
And expecting different results'?
I repeatedly looked in the same places,
Of course, to no avail.
The last thing I wrote with the gold plated pen
Was amendments to my fourth book, 'Beyond the Cave.'
I didn't write a sonnet, or any kind of poem,
Just grammatical amendment notes:
Rather an anti-climax.
Will the gold plated pen show up?
Sometimes lost objects have a habit of popping up
Least expected.
I sure hope so.
What I have found though,
In the three hours after realizing it has gone,
Is I still can write,
That the gold plated pen didn't have any magical powers
Like Thor's Hammer.
I'm writing this with a stainless steel pen
And the words flow just the same.

24-3-18

(I found it a year later down the side of my bed. I was most happy!)

Bats in the belfry
Flying free
Though it's too dark
For you to see.

28-3-18

The sky smiles
Through the bare branches,
The branches
Like the capillaries
Of a human brain,
A human brain
Enmeshed in woodland.

28-3-18

The dawn chorus
Celebrates
The return
Of their vision.

28-3-18

Aeschylus snoozing upright like Buddha
By a babbling brook.
He sighs as he recalls the vision of Dionysus
Manifesting and cajoling him to be a playwright.
Dionysus, wild visage, god of wine and ecstasy,
Waxes lyrical in his persuasiveness,
Wild hands gesticulating in frenzy.

High above, on a big wind,
An eagle,
Wings akimbo, soaring on a thermal,
Clutching a tortoise in large talons.
The soaring eagle intends to drop the flailing tortoise
From a great height smashing its shell
Against a rock so it can devour the soft flesh beneath.
The soaring eagle, high above, sees a rock below
Shining in the midday sun.
The eagle drops the tortoise…

The tortoise silently screams as it plummets to earth…
The tortoise, severe impact, smashes against Aeschylus' head
And kills the renowned playwright instantly.
The eagle had mistook Aeschylus' bald head for a rock.

28-3-18

PAPER

Infinitesimally thin but contains facets of my soul.
My soul, solid, but I feel self-conscious of my flaws.
Flimsy fibers firmly connected reaches out to others.
Do I try too hard and fall embarrassingly short?
Ink, letters, taken generations to evolve.
Precariously balanced morale grimaces at the world.

29-3-18

Sparks fly from her wild hair,
Profound smile spiritually rare,
Unique dance of notable flair,
Her eyes beam igniting air,
All compelled to stand and stare.

4-4-18

I welcomed clement spring, greeting snowdrops,
My smiling eyes in a butterfly dance.
The frisky foxes survived another harsh grey winter.
The undulating hills animated in verdure
Bringing me in contact with heaven.
The fire in my soul rekindled,
Passion, motivation and energy to walk for miles.
Here I was at the venerable poet's village, Helpstone.
I have read his delightful poetry, now I, grateful pilgrim,
Walk the cottage rooms he grew up in.
I feel a spiritual connection, an affinity.
In the nearby church I respectfully stand silently over his grave.
Your poetry, John Clare, will live eternally.

6-4-18

When I was a child I had my mouth sewn shut.
The silence dwelt within my gut.
My ears pulsed with all the noise
Of chattering confident girls and boys.
Fear followed me wherever I walked.
They thought me foolish, my inability to talk.
I watched them with my verbose eyes.
I was invisible though standing nigh.
But as I grew I knew what to do,
Assert myself or they wouldn't have a clue
Who I was, the boy inside.
It's lonely amongst people when you hide.
At 16 I left school, thrown amongst men.
The silence started all over again.
With the lads my age I made friends,
But the blokes, I could not relate to them.
But as I grew I knew what to do,
Assert myself or they wouldn't have a clue
Who I was, the man inside.
It's lonely amongst people when you hide.

6-4-18

FRED HOYLE'S ANALOGY REGARDING ABIOGENESIS

The old junk yard, old dilapidated cars, tyres, windscreens, leaky engine oil, cables, leather seats, pvc seats, dials, pedals, buckets, copper pipes, brass pipes, plastic pipes, the old junk yard, piles of twisted metal, iron, steel, aluminium, towering cars piled on top of each other without doors, electrical components waiting to pulse into life...

The tornado fiercely spinning, violently twisting, blowing, rasping, howling, angry yelling force hits the old junk yard like a battering ram, twisted metal spinning in the vortex, the junk yard's contents violently twirling, metal clattering, metal battering in protest, spinning.

The tornado moves on...

There, in the old junk yard, by random chance, constructed by the tornado, sitting proudly, is a jumbo jet.

11-4-18

GRIMES

I first saw her on a desert road.
Her arms were swaying like the wind.
A yellow snake draped around her neck.
Large shining eyes inviting me in.

The next time was in a stadium.
Her dance and song instantly charmed.
She behaved natural and spontaneous.
I watched her feeling soothing calm.

Her live shows began with solo and synth.
Fan of Dune sings haunting melody.
Her concentration at the decks evinced
She was possessed by music entirely.

Her high kicks from rigorous ballet training.
Her dancers with unique slick moves.
Emotional performance shows she's not feigning.
Her vampire teeth snarl at you.

15-4-18

I am for the loners, the down and outs, the quiet ones.
I am for the vulnerable, the bullied, the gentle ones.
I am for the victim, the scapegoat, the innocent.
I am for the self-conscious, the insecure, the socially awkward.
I am for the poverty stricken, the disease ridden, those who are hidden.
I am for the lonely, the depressed, the suicidal.
I am for the life savers, the carers, the humanitarians.
I am for the musicians, poets and artists.
I am for those who love so much they are a little obsessed.
I am for the spurned, the unrequited, the dispossessed.
I am for those who turn disability into victory.
I am for the 'defeated' who try their best.
I am for those who do not quite fit in.
They all have large hearts like Oz's man of tin.

17-4-18

It's our duty, as human beings,
To develop, evolve, recognise our potential,
Become the authentic self.
It is not always easy
When we're trapped in a system,
Dictated by circumstance,
Used to a certain way of life.
The people around us
Can either stifle us, or help let us grow.
To make a positive change,
A conscious effort to adopt new habits,
Behaviour that suits who we want to be,
To learn new skills,
Should be, despite the challenges,
A permanent way of life.

17-4-18

My glistening tears fill the shadowy room.
My inveterate despair like a loom
Weaves a pall of inscrutable darkness.
I will master myself...
The past dithering despondent Hamlet no more.
The nadir of my life will not return.
The futility of existence is an illusion
Created by those who have lost their way.
The razor blade sucking the weeping vein
Will transmogrify into the divine music of hope.
Years of desperation and cynicism crumble,
And glorious towers, refulgent beacons
Of gleaming light scan the land
And replenish durable life.

21-4-18

A bumble bee was the only living creature
I had seen in three years.
Its gossamer translucent iridescent wings
Vibrated in the sultry morning air.
Its furry yellow and black abdomen
Bristled under a golden sun.
Its buzz was the only language I knew.
The regal creature settled on my palm
And crawled around tickling my nerve endings,
Antennae twitching.
'Little bee,' I whispered, 'go forth
And make love to the glorious flowers.
They need your industrious expertise
To help them grow and multiply.'
With that the bumble bee ascended
Into the clear blue sky and zigzagged away
To ply its valuable trade and fill its pollen basket.

22-4-18

My face is the tip of an iceberg:
Surface belies thought.
Last night, in ecstatic dream,
Far out above a stormy ocean,
I was a raging torrent,
Growling, howling and laughing
At utter latitude,
At one with primeval elements,
Utter joy being a storm,
Wild with waves,
Away from civil constraints.

24-4-18

I know an exotic flower
On a distant planet
That if you look upon it
Unmoved and indifferent
You walk away unaffected.

But if you espy
The flower's incredible beauty
And admire its efflorescence,
You become poisoned
And wither away.

27-4-18

The worm is slithering underground.
The blackbird is in the grass searching for the worm.
The worm can feel the vibrations of the blackbird
And knows it is there.
The blackbird can hear the slithering worm.
PECK!
The blackbird pulls the head of the worm
And its long slimy body slithers from the mud.
The blackbird, merciless, ravenous,
Grasps the wiggling writhing worm in its beak.
The worm screams in mute horror,
Its nerve endings twitch
In stark realisation it is
To be devoured alive.

29-4-18

Sparkling blue planet is a miracle in space.
Refulgent sun blesses harmonious human race.
Volumes speak silent mystic trees.
Soothing psyche the humming bumblebee.
A barren desert has been my wretched mind,
Oblivious to the moon's silver shine.
Undulating ocean cools my boiling blood.
As my skin so grains of wood.
The baboon is in my antediluvian bones.
The mountains edified my thirsty soul.
Epiphany in the incorporeal grin.
I searched outside for that within.

29-4-18

I walked past a guy selling *The Big Issue.* I stopped to talk to him. Because he was so used to being ignored tears welled up in his eyes and he thanked me for noticing him. I was holding books and so was he. He proceeded to tell me about the book he was reading. It turned out he liked fantasy novels. I told him I had written one. We arranged for me to drop my book off, *Gorky,* at the nearby chippy so he could pick it up. Later I heard he was enjoying the book.

3-5-18

I called my fourth book *Beyond the Cave* as a reference to Plato. He believed in another world, possibly ethereal, where there are perfect forms: eg. triangle, circle, cat, horse, essence of beauty etc. We, in our corporeal state, see only simulacrums or poor representations of the absolute. He utilizes the analogy of the cave to elucidate his philosophical theory: a man who has permanently lived in a cave sees only shadows on the wall (shadows merely indicate) of what lays outside and believes the shadows to be the objects themselves. As a poet and philosopher, I am trying to hone my rudimentary perception to see deeper and more acutely into the world.

3-5-18

Let's be leisurely
And spend the day
How we please,
Because when
You're in the rat race
It can drag you
To your knees.

3-5-18

OUTSIDE THE WINDOW

The blackbird and his wife
Do not take long to notice
The grape, apple and plum.
First Mr Blackbird,
For that is the pecking order.
If she tries to eat first
He aggressively shoos her away.
I put the food in the same place
Every time.
They must monitor the area regularly.
Blackbirds have to accommodate human movement.
The sky is cerulean blue,
Just a slight wisp of cloud.
The sun is welcome after a day of rain.
A seagull confidently glides past;
A pigeon moves from roof top to roof top;
A sparrow zooms from the hedge.
The birds in the vicinity
Are not particularly colourful
But fascinating nevertheless.
It is 5.45pm and in an hour
I will order Chinese takeaway.

My eating will be less hurried than the birds.
They don't know when their next meal
Is coming from
Or who will interrupt their feed.
As they eat, their heads
Swivel in jerky movements
Continually on the alert
For predators and interlopers.
I see a child walking down the street
Head buried in Iphone oblivious to surroundings.
I read for three hours this morning,
Then practised guitar and harmonica.
I'm more inclined to practise now I have an electronic tuning
device.
My guitar looks more aesthetically pleasing
Now each string is the correct note.
Subsequently, I feel slightly more harmonious too.

3-5-18

She summons
A fire
In her soul
That blazes
Through
Her eyes.

I know enough
To know
I want
To know her.

6-5-18

Butterfly flying
High in the sky
Why do you
Have to die?

6-5-18

It's May day holiday weekend.
The beach is replete with sun worshippers.
There are rows of glittering parked cars.
Little children cradle muddy parcels
Of sand as if it's treasure.
There's a jovial cry of 'Happy Sunday!'
With an affirmative reply of 'Happy Sunday!'.

11-5-18

Society never wanted me.
It always pushed me to the edge.
But I waited patiently
And always adhered to my pledge.

So while they closed their doors,
I kept on reading books.
I got used to being ignored.
Society didn't give a fuck.

But my personal progress
Was always assured.
I kept on trying my best.
I read more and more.

Now I think they're ridiculous
Never acknowledging me.
But I don't need their validation.
The reward is what I read.

11-5-18

A child said my poem was good.
I've learnt some guitar chords.
My fingering on recorder improves.
I bend notes on the harmonica whilst playing the blues.
The cover of my new book was emailed today:
It looks very good, effective, I must say.
I weight trained in the garden
Whilst my skin turned brown.
I keep on my toes as I walk in town.
I maintain fascination for everything I do.
My self-esteem remains solid.
Life is a privilege, I reflect, when the day is through.

11-5-18

MANY
MISCONCEPTIONS

My name is Luna.
The kids at school call me 'Looney'.
I kinda don't mind, it's usually good-natured.
But then a giant wart grew on the end of my nose.
Horror to be subjected to such a conspicuous disfigurement.
The kids called me 'Warty.'
This time it was not such gentle ribbing.
They became quite malicious.
It started to get me down.
I went to the doctor:
He prescribed a cream,
Which removed it for a while,
But much to my disappointment it grew back.
It became unbearable.
I looked in the mirror
And there was the huge ugly
Wart like a beacon on the end of my nose.

My name is Luna.
I worship the moon.
I bathe in the moon's silvery rays.
I acquire wisdom from the moon's silence.
I opened my book of witchcraft:
A spell for removing warts.
Contrary to popular myth,
Witches don't usually have warts.
I rubbed my wart with chicken liver,
Uttered a mystic incantation,
And placed the liver in the brown earth
Of an ancient forest
As the tree spirits melodiously sang.
As the chicken liver decomposed in the ground,
My wart began to shrink,
Until it was finally gone.
The wart never appeared again.
I worship the moon.
My name is Luna,
But the kids call me 'Loony.'

11-5-18

One night a wolf wagged her tail at me.

The next night an owl twood as a wing feather fell into my hands.

The next night an adder coiled around my ankle and fell to sleep.

The next night the lake whispered ancient secrets as I played violin.

The next night a tree spirit advised me how to stay happy.

The next night, the night itself implanted in my mind forever pleasant dreams.

The stars, the moon, the meteorites and comets, shine direct into my eyes

Imbuing me with the celestial light of the heavens.

15-5-18

I was looking for my hat,
But I had it in my hand.
I hope you understand,
It does not make me daft.
I was looking for my hat,
But it was in my hand.
I don't mind if you laugh.

17-5-18

TONGUE
IN CHEEK
STEREOTYPING

Inspired by reading Balzac's description of Parisian life.

A typical Grimberian always carries a haddock in their pocket which they can gnaw on if they are peckish at any time. They ardently support Grimsby Town FC but hardly go to watch them and cannot tell you where they in the league. They all used to work on the fish docks and lament that the place is now a ghost town. They all moved into the fish finger factories but still believe they are dockers. It is a well known fact that Grimberians drink more alcohol than anyone else in the world. Go to any pub at any time of the day and night and you find a hoard of them suckling on a pint of larger like a lion cub on a teat. Grimberians believe anyone who lives outside Grimsby is a foreigner. The border between Grimsby and the outside is more impenetrable than the Berlin wall and you require special papers to enter the town. To be a Grimberian you must say the word 'fuck' in every sentence. If you don't say the word 'fuck' in every sentence you're not hard enough. When riding a cycle in Grimsby it is required you hold a fag in one hand and a can of beer in the other, though how we steer is a mystery we wish not to divulge. Grimberians always watch Coronation Street and talk about it as if it's real. But of course, the description of Grimberians I have just given is not real, 'cause I'm a Grimberian and I'm nothing like that!

17-5-18

I think I wanted to be like my uncle Jeff.
Happy go lucky. Always smiling.
He never seemed to worry. Always lived for today.
He would playfully pull on his mam's
(My grandma's) apron strings;
Grandma would always wear a hat indoors:
I would playfully take it off her head,
Which seemed to amuse her
And slightly annoy her at the same time.
In the 60s Uncle Jeff was into The Beatles;
He had a mop top haircut
And all the records.
Uncle Jeff's sister, Janice, recalls happy days
On Cleethorpes beach swimming with him.
They were both members of Cleethorpes Canoe Club:
Uncle Jeff built a canoe from wood and canvas
Using the proper plans,
And made a very good job of it,
Which they would row around the pier.
I remember when I was aged 7 I lived at my grandmas for the
summer
While my mam was in hospital.
I told him I had Cadbury soldiers, I meant cavalry soldiers:
This amused him a lot.
That summer he said, 'Cup your hands':
I did, puzzled why he said such a thing,
And he poured loads of loose change filling my hands up.
I'll never forget that. I thought I was rich.
I bought loads of sweets.
Uncle Jeff started as a brickie's labourer,
But then became a qualified mechanic.

He drove a Mini and motorbikes.
He once saw a gang of blokes harassing a woman,
She was being dragged into a car,
And he went to protect her.
He was beat up, unconscious, in a gutter, nose broken.
He told his sister, Aunt Janice, 'I've just met the woman I'm
going to marry:
Auntie Karen.
He would say to my mam with his broad smile:
'How's my favourite sister-in-law?'
When I was a little older, Uncle Jeff asked me what my
favourite band was:
I cannot remember my reply,
But I asked him what his was, he said, 'Wizard.'
He gave me a bowling badge with the word 'Excel' on it,
And I proudly wore it on my uniform all the way through
school.

He died at the age of 25 in a motoring accident.
His moped hit a lorry head on and killed him instantly.
I vividly remember when they phoned my dad
To give him the tragic news.
They say the best die young.

When he died, our family received all his 45s:
I was very young but it was a revelation to me,
The first time I remember music in our house:
I particularly remember playing The Beatles *Paperback Writer,*
Rolling Stones *Get of my Cloud,* The Kinks *You Really Got me,*
Del Shannon *Runaway.*
I played those records over and over again…

17-5-18

There was this virtual woman
Living in my starved mind.
I imagined high compatibility
And growing happiness in eternity.
We would develop understanding of each other
And cultivate our love.
But then shock! I saw this virtual woman
With a virtual man.
I denied it at first,
But rationally realised *their* high compatibility:
So I reluctantly relinquished my pre-occupation.
Now there is a void where the virtual woman
Used to be,
And I am now empty and far less happy.

19-5-18

I am Zeus.
I tell the truth.
They are proof
There is no roof
On spoof.

28-5-18

MEMORY FROM BEING TWO YEAR'S OLD.

Stepping from posh car.
I'm all dressed up.
These aren't the clothes I usually wear.
I'm all smart.
I like being all smart.
The girl next to me
(The bridesmaid)
Is dressed like a fairy.
She is pretty.
I like the girl next to me.
Through the ceremony
I am holding her hand.
I like holding her hand.
It makes me happy.
The wedding is over.
The girl is leaving.
Oh no! Don't go!
I'm hurting.
I feel like crying.
The girl has gone.
I'm really hurting!
No one knows how I feel.

28-5-18

I'm gonna rip off these fetters
That society has clasped on my brain.
I'm gonna roar like a gorilla,
Beat my chest,
And snap my chain.

31-5-18

The
Ladder
Is
Long;
The
Ladder
Is
Steep:
Nobody
Knows
Where
The
Ladder
Will
Lead.

31-5-18

I want to tell you about my poetry.
Compared to you I might write differently.
I try vary my subject and style.
I try make you think; I try make you smile.
You may think it has merit; you may think it no good.
I write about the sun, moon, sea and the woods.
I write about unrequited love.
I write about when I laced on boxing gloves.
I write about death. I write about hope.
I write about my past struggles to cope.
Revealing yourself can leave you vulnerable.
I like to think most poets are honourable.
I realise we can all build walls.
We open up when the muse calls.
I'm only in competition with myself.
I improve my writing by reading a book from the shelf.
I could easily hide all day long,
Telling myself I'll never belong:
My neighbour knows my neighbour better than me:
Though reason tells me this is mere fallacy.
We all, I guess, have an element of insecurity.
We only open up with familiarity.
Social convention dictates how to behave.
Social anxiety can make you feel less brave.
A kind smile, a kind word, and I am saved.
Nobody really knows what others are going through.
Sometimes you may feel isolated too.
I have reasons to be cheerful when I have health,
Worth more than all the material wealth.
I've had my share of suicidal fights.
I will never relinquish reaching for the light.
Little acts of kindness can stop us feeling blue.
I will never stop believing in you.

2-6-18

My piss is conspiring against me.
It won't excrete in one smooth stream.
It scatters like a watering device for grass.
Now I have piss stains all over me pants.
Fuck, now I'm gonna have to walk into the bar,
Facing a few chuckles, and a few ha ha's.
I know, I'll stay in the bog all night.
No, no, they'll know something's not right.
Oh well, here goes, conspicuous stain high viz.
Mmm, no one notices: it's only me conscious of my piss.
Nevertheless, to conceal it I'll try.
Cross my legs till the fucker dries.

2-6-18

You know the jerk, the berk, the one who tries to work you up.
Don't take the bait.
Don't lapse into hate.
It may not be your fate to be their mate:
But ain't that great!
Don't get into a skunk fight with a skunk.
Don't bear a grudge or take the hump.
Don't let it weigh you down.
Don't let them make you frown.
Smile and be friendly in ignorant's face.
Set an example in the place.
Don't let them dominate you, complicate you.
Don't let them shake your world when they try to blame you.
Aim higher, don't stop trying.
Life is better if you deny them.
Why they do it, who can tell?
They would change paradise into hell.
They would make a saint swear.
It's not your problem they don't care.
Ultimately, they have to live with themselves.
It must be mayhem in their shell.
Just say, oh well!
What do they see in their reflection?
Do they ever heed any lessons?
Do they ever grow as a human being?
Are they totally incapable of seeing?

2-6-18

PETRARCHAN SONNET

My silent love has to remain concealed.
To speak of my love would drive you away.
You turn night in my mind to sunny day.
I would love to inform you how I feel.
Risking aloofness ensures my lips sealed.
I can anticipate what you might say:
'No thank you, I cannot possibly stay'
Would be the price I pay for being real.
I will be contented at being friends,
Enjoy your company when you are near,
A beautiful woman who speaks to me.
You oblivious how my soul you mend.
Somehow I will convey how much I care,
Though there will never be intimacy.

14-6-18

SHAKESPEARIAN SONNET

I roam through life an isolated soul.
I resign to it always being so.
Glowing love lives like an underground mole.
Maybe she has guessed and already knows.
I am always friendly and kind to her.
Perhaps sometimes going beyond the line.
Cautiously telling her how much I care.
She may not know how she makes me feel fine.
Inappropriate to lay my soul bare.
Do you notice my smile and shining eyes?
Can you see how I struggle to behave?
Is holding back no more than cautious lies?
Is there light and love beyond the dank cave?
I will get on with life to distract me.
Though I know the coast is kissed by the sea.

14-6-18

SPENSERIAN
SONNET

When a rose dies another takes its place.
A small bird from an egg hatches in spring.
After a frown comes a smile on the face.
After it's fledged the bird is on the wing.
Eternity's symbol shines golden ring.
Let's be in tune with nature's steady pace.
Outside the window all birds sweetly sing.
The trees soothe my spirit dancing in air.
There's an elemental force everywhere.
Tap into the energy, raise your soul.
For every flower is comely and fair.
Each shimmering petal makes up the whole.
Impressive mandala becomes our psyche.
Be as free as the river darting pike.

14-6-18

She can have the fierceness
Of an implacable demon,
Or the gentle joy
Of a smiling flower.

14-6-18

'She's lost control' Joy Division

I fell in love too quick
So she gave me the slip.
She was an angel,
Though she had her wings clipped.
She sipped whisky
In the bars down town,
Slept around.
She slips into many guises.
She's full of many surprises.
But she's lost grip,
As she pouts her lips
And wiggles her hips,
She's lost grip.
She found herself
In bed with the bad.
When she died,
Everyone was sad.

19-6-18

Under a full bloodshot moon
Amongst fierce crackling lightning
In the eerie shadowy woods
Amidst enormous imposing silhouettes
Is a budgie.

19-6-18

When I saw those UFOs
Flashing in the night sky
I realised the front door
Of my house was so flimsy.

23-6-18

DREAM

It was dawn, or was it dusk?
Me and an old school friend stood by the park.
The clouds were grey, dark, dense and low.
We flew kites, soaring in the louring sky,
But such was the low dense clouds
We could not see our kites soaring into the louring sky.
I thought best to pull the kites in
For it was futile to see only string.
And instantly, I thought of messaging you
And tell you of the events.
I derived great comfort that you would know.
Then I awoke…

23-6-18

TRUE

Buckets of larger on a warm Corfu night.
Me and my mate met two girls.
We conga back to their hotel in the sultry dark,
Making our own music.
We entered their room,
And I, drunk, slumped on her bed.
Then, suddenly, two boys from the room next door walked in.
I, disappointed, decided not to stay.
I staggered to the balcony.
All I could see was pitch dark outside.
I thought I was on the ground floor
So jumped over the side,
Falling, falling, thinking, this is not good.
In my drunken haze I had forgotten
We had walked up a flight of stairs.
Falling, falling, into the dark… BANG!
I hit the concrete floor like a rag doll.
If I had not been so drunk I would not have been so loose,
Which saved me with only minor lesions.
My friend poked his head over the balcony
And said, 'What did you do that for?'

27-6-18

The last time I was in Westminster Abbey
Was with the delightful lady, Rupa.
I made straight for Poet's Corner,
She was more interested in the tombs
Of the kings and queens,
And, alas, we went our separate ways.

23-6-18

THE ABSURDITY
OF TRYING TOO
HARD TO BE
DIFFERENT

As we walked along the beach,
Sea breeze in our hair,
My two friends jovially sang,
'Oh I do like to be beside the seaside,'
Whilst I sullenly and silently dragged my feet
Alongside them
Wearing an ironic smile.

But as soon as my two friends
Indulged in earnest debate
About a weighty political issue,
I started singing a silly song.

26-6-18

ZIMBARDO

They glued a top hat onto a sloth
To observe its behaviour,
And it became more cabaret.

26-8-18

The sky was clear and unadulterated blue.
The glowing sun warmly shone on us both.
We were laying by a margin of a pellucid lake,
Fragments of sunlight danced on the surface.
Around us we could hear a zephyr stroking the trees.
I looked into her speaking eyes.
She smiled and looked so very happy.
I returned her smile tinged with sadness.
She looked completely happy,
A complete happiness that only a good person could feel.
I was both good and bad and could not fully share her joy
For I felt I did not deserve such a gift.
I wanted to be happy for her happiness,
And to an extent I was.
I did not resent her happiness
For that would mean too much distance between us.
So I tried to understand her happiness,
Tried to be pleased for her happiness.
As my appreciation grew,
I became to believe I could be a better man.
She made me feel I could be good,
And as this belief grew,
The distance between me and her decreased.
I grew nearer to this divine female spirit.
She made me feel a joy I never thought I'd feel.

26-6-18

The starlings,
In one graceful swoop,
Divested the lawn of bread.

The starlings,
Like a gang from Westside Story,
Aggressively descend
Do the devour dance
And instantly decimate the bread.

30-6-18

Call me
What number
You like,
I'll still
Be Mike.

30-6-18

I am the Roman Emperor, Laborious.
Get down on your knees… Stand up…
Get down on your knees… Stand up…
Get down on your knees… Stand up…
Get down on your knees… Stand up…

30-6-18

She put something in her pocket,
But she forgot it…
It grew into a universe,
Swirling galaxies,
Billions of glowing suns,
Planets with oceans and trees,
And on one of those planets,
You and me.

30-6-18

He has lived under
A black cloud all his life,
And tried to drag
Everyone else under it.

30-6-18

Sound of jet fighter.
What's that mode of transport, Zigglix?
It is to transport bombs, Zogglox.
Bombs, Zigglix?
Bombs, yes, the humans tend to blow each other up, Zogglox.
Mmm, curious past time, Zigglix.
Yes, Zogglox.

2-7-18

VARANUS KOMODOENSIS

Buffalo, basking in the Indonesian mud,
Finding welcome shade in the merciless heat of the day,
Lolling, half asleep in shallow water and mud,
Flies buzzing relentlessly swarming around torso and head.
Komodo dragon, many times smaller,
Aggressive dinosaur instinct,
With atavistic reptilian eye sees the buffalo,
And driven by insatiable hunger
Is drawn to the dozing buffalo.
The buffalo not excessively bothered
By this smaller creature.
Komodo persistently harasses buffalo.
Komodo dominates a physically superior animal.
Komodo is wary of buffalo horns and kick
And like a boxer keeps just out of range.
Komodo strikes, bites buffalo leg.
Blood pours from the wound.
Other komodos are alerted by blood,
Lust for blood, blood frenzy,
And together attack the buffalo.
The buffalo despondently limps away.
Six komodos avidly pursue the distressed limping buffalo.

Komodos tenaciously follow buffalo where ever it goes.
Day after day, komodos watch, waiting,
While venom gradually seeps through buffalo's veins.
The komodos wait for weeks
As the buffalo is gradually drained of strength
From reptilian toxins.
Komodos patiently watching the buffalo,
Biding their time.
Then, overnight, the hapless buffalo succumbs to poison and
dies.
Six komodos in a few hours' feeding frenzy
With powerful jaws twist flesh
Stripping meat to the bones.
All that is left of the buffalo,
Laying there,
Is skeletal remains
And the relentless buzzing swarming flies.

2-7-18

Animals evolved
Aggressive traits
In order to compete
For resources:
Hence, war is nothing
More than
Animalistic behaviour.

2-7-18

The stars sat
In anticipation
Of your discernment:
They gleefully
Scintillate
For your smiling eyes.

2-7-18

I'm left behind.
I missed the train.
I've got to sit out
In the rain.

3-7-18

Inspired by *'Fear no more the heat o' th' sun'*
by William Shakespeare

Worry not about money.
Worry not about having to try.
Worry not if she loves you.
It's time to ascend into the sky.

Worry not about their indifference.
Worry not about refugees' plight.
Worry not about the future.
It's time to ascend into the sky.

Worry not about hatred.
Worry not about lies.
Worry not about anger.
It's time to ascend into the sky.

Worry not about leaders.
Worry not about excessive pride.
Worry not about selfishness.
It's time to ascend into the sky.

Worry not about virulent disease.
Worry not about why.
Worry not about war.
It's time to ascend into the sky.

3-7-18

She travels America in a car.
She plays in all the music bars.
She's a blues wizard, a shining star.
She played so sweetly
A bluejay perched
On her guitar.

3-7-18

There were three men
Trying to attract
The same woman.

The first man,
In order to impress her,
Filled his house with shit.

The second man,
In order to impress her,
Filled his house with gold.

The third man,
In order to impress her,
Filled his house with flowers.

The time came
For the woman
To inspect each house:
First, the house
The man filled with shit.
She was not impressed one bit.

Second, the house
The man filled with gold.
It left her feeling cold.

Then she went
To the house
Of the man who filled it with flowers.
She imagined, with this man,
Passing pleasant hours.

5-7-18

I feel most free
When I'm hitting my free-standing punch bag
In the back garden.
This July morning, in the glorious sun,
With just my shorts on,
I'm tenaciously fighting for the championship of the world.
54 years old, well past my best,
They said the come-back was foolhardy,
But like Rocky Balboa, I defy the odds.
Physical expression, release of aggression,
Sweat oozing, heart pounding,
Giving my opponent a lesson
Gulping the warm summer air.
My range is good, still got technique,
Power in punches, feeling sharp,
Though stamina ain't what it was,
But I feel free.
And afterwards, to slake parched mouth,
I eat ice cold grapefruit in natural juices from a tin,
Most refreshing.
Endorphins pump through my body,
A satisfying ache in my muscles,
A superior high to drugs.

6-7-18

PLOGGER'S FIELD

I've played golf,
Took a swing,
Snapped the club in half,
And gave it back to me mate
(It was his)
On here.

I've played cricket,
Pretty badly,
On here.

I've played rugby
With my school friends
Practising for the local championships
On here.

I've played football,
In the sun, rain and snow,
On here.

I've been laid on me back,
Drunk,
Wondering what the fuck I'm doing here,
On here.

9-7-18

Oblivious
To the resplendent
Shimmering roses
Nearby
He stooped
To pick up
A pound coin.

11-7-18

Valkyries, hear my plea,
Pluck me from the battlefield.
I can't fight no more.
Both arms are chopped off.
I only have one leg.
And one of my eyeballs is on the floor.

11-7-18

W.I. SPECIFIC
POEM

I was walking down the street
On a bright sunny day
When a man stood in my way
And said, 'Hold out your palm.'
His eyes glowed like the sun
And I was compelled to comply.
He placed a tiny seed in my palm.
He said, 'Place this seed in your garden.
Press it into the soil.
Water it and watch it grow.
You will not be disappointed.'
So I did what the man said.
I placed the unremarkable seed in the soil.
I gently watered it with summer rain
Collected in my watering can.
The first day there was a shoot.
The second day there was a branch.
The third day there was an avalanche of leaves.
The fourth day, much to my surprise,
Was a jam jar hanging from a stalk.
I plucked the jam jar
And it donged like a church bell.
It was filled with what seemed to be jam.
I brought the jar into the kitchen,
Unscrewed the lid

And an amazing fragrant aroma imbued the room.
With a gleaming knife
I spread a dollop of jam onto a slice of bread.
The deep red jam magically glistened on the bread.
I took a cautious bite.
It was the most succulent strawberry jam I had ever eaten.
I quickly rushed to the plant
To see if I could pluck more jam jars from it.
Sure enough, there were jam jars
Of various colours hanging from the branches
Sparkling like the stars.
I plucked each one from the bush:
Dong! Dong! Dong!
I opened the lids and tasted each one:
Blackberry, raspberry, marmalade,
Lemon curd, strawberry, blueberry,
Apple and plum.
Each flavour tasted divine.
How lucky, I thought, to possess a jam plant!

11-7-18

The starlings all perch around
The bird bath fighting each other
And no one ends up getting a drink:
It's a little like humans
Fighting for a piece of land,
Blowing it up
So it's no use to anybody.

23-7-18

Red wine:
In the evening
Her mouth
Is turned up;
In the morning
Her mouth
Is turned down.

23-7-18

Today I saw a sparrow
Feeding another sparrow
And I felt such joy.
A mother
Feeding its
Little girl or boy.

23-7-18

I name the spider Sid, after Sid Vicious. Sid died tragically young,
and so did Sid. Sid was a thorn in the side of society, but Sid wasn't.

The spider was like an animal:
I've seen smaller mammals.
The huge spider,
The magnificent spider,
The most incredible house spider
That ever lived,
With magical legs in sync
Crawled into the vulnerable open air,
And with one swift stamp of his foot
The monarch of insects
Was reduced to a forlorn puddle on the tiles.

23-7-18

I rely on you;
You rely on me:
Let's sit down
And have a chat
With a cup of tea.

23-7-18

You sit there in your central heated meeting room
On your plush chair
Drinking the finest water money can buy
Waxing lyrical about policies and procedures,
What you've done, what you're doing, and what you're going to do,
Whilst the tramp sits on the park bench
With no where to go,
Water seeping through his clothes,
Shoes with poking toes,
Mental health deteriorating,
Then you go to your luxurious home
In your all expenses paid taxi
Via the takeaway.

25-7-18

A BETRAYAL
OF TRUST

The otter,
Never seeing a man before,
Came to feed from the man's hand:
That was his first mistake,
And his last.
The man saw the otter's fur
And thought: 'That will look good on me.'

25-7-18

And buzzy
came in,
A bluebottle
As big
As a big toe
Buzzing
Like the revving
Of a drag car.

25-7-18

The spectre
Is inspecting you
Expecting you
To behave,
And you better
If you want
To be saved.

25-7-18

On the back,
Pat, pat, pat,
But you always
Ignore the facts.

25-7-18

I can't watch a girl in a tutu
Without feeling blue.
I can't watch a girl in a tutu
Without eyes of dew.
I can't watch a girl in a tutu
Without thinking of you.
I wonder what your life was
In ballerina school.

26-7-18

The surface water undulated, rippled towards the shore,
An eerie silhouette skating along the bed.
The deer calf frolicking in the shallows of the calm sea.
The killer whale senses the contrasting water tensions, smells food
And like a missile relentlessly hurtles towards the shore
Breaking the surface leaving frothy foam in its wake.
Is the baby deer aware it is prey?
The calf seems to try and runaway, but water resistance, hinders.
Smooth as a jet plane quick as an arrow effortlessly cutting through the water
The killer whale is getting closer, closer, closer!
Mother dear, doe, from the coast,
Sees the dire situation and without hesitation leaps into the perilous sea
Bounding between baby calf and giant predator.
The selfless doe has made herself a food barrier between calf and whale.
With one snap of his powerful jaws
The doe is submerged, gone!
I look on in dismay, incredulous to what took place.

26-7-18

PENETRATION
BEYOND COLOUR

When I first met her
All I could see was her skin,
Then I got to talk to her
And all I could see was her eyes.

28-7-18

Vaughn Williams
'Lark Rising'
Conveys majestically
The delightful bird
Ascending
From the tree,
The same tree
The Stradivarius
Was made from.

28-7-18

I went
To drama school
For three years, then,
I was really pleased,
I got my first role,
As the back end
Of a horse.

28-7-18

Why do you fill the kettle
To the brim
When you're only having two cups?
You're waiting 20 minutes
For the kettle to boil
And using all the electric up.

28-7-18

So the monkey is in a little cage,
And he sign languages to indifferent passers by
About his life in the jungle,
How he loves girl monkey
And his two babies,
His resourcefulness
Foraging for food
And knows all the edible plants,
How he knows the best places to go for water,
How he plays in the trees swinging freely,
Then a human buys him
And eats his brain
Whilst he is still alive,
Monkey's last sign is,
'Why?'

28-7-18

ETHOLOGY

Observing
Wildlife
Elucidates
Human
Behaviour.

28-7-18

Truth
Is
Immutable;
Change
Is
Inevitable.

28-7-18

In winter
They complain
It's cold;
In summer
They complain
It's hot:
They're never satisfied
With what they've got.

28-7-18

Born on feet with adequate awareness.
Danger lurks in every shadow.
The calf is running
Soon after birth.
Calf instantly recognises
The insatiable hunger
In the wolf's eyes,
It's gnashing teeth.
To evade the predator
Calf already has sufficient speed.

30-7-18

Do not bind
The independent mind:
That would
Be unkind.

30-7-18

When all that sophisticated technology
Was monitoring and assessing his physiology,
The rudimentary question still needed to be asked:
'How are you feeling?'

31-7-18

A fish frenetically swims away from a shark,
Probably in high anxiety,
So a behaviourist could presumably conclude
Fish have feelings.

31-7-18

Koi carp, confined in a little tank,
Stationary, looking depressed;
Transferred to a commodious pond
Swimming rapidly enjoying flexing fins.

31-7-18

WITH LIBERTY COMES RESPONSIBILITY

Someone walked on a fragile roof
Just to demonstrate they were free.

31-7-18

Look at
the hooligans
on the pitch
As they riot.

Look at
the horses
Grazing
in the field,
So quiet.

1-8-18

Here she comes
Graceful gait
Amongst
The ancient trees.
I'm contented as
She sits
Next to me,
Basking in the sun.
Musical girl.
Guitar girl.
Song girl.
Here she lays
On the shimmering
Summer grass
And stretches
Her dainty limbs
As I read
My hasty
Cobbled together
Poetry.

2-8-18

Hillosophy:
The philosophy
Of climbing hills.

2-8-18

TRANSFORMATION OF PERCEPTION

So me, my girlfriend, mate and his girlfriend, went to Skegness.
We sat in a cafe almost in silence.
I stared out the window and thought, there's got to be somewhere better than this.
And we went into the arcades, played all the games, but I felt no fun,
Just passing time, and I thought, there's got to be somewhere better than this.
And we went to the Funfair, there was screeching and bells,
Sirens and wailing, and it reminded me of hell,
And we went on all the rides, and I hardly smiled,
And I thought, there's got to be somewhere better than this.
And we went on the beach, but it was out of reach,
I had never read a poem to connect me,
And I thought, there's got to be somewhere better than this,
Because I was ill-equipped to appreciate the scene.
And now I've read poetry and philosophy,
The spiritual minds of the past, the thinkers, contemplatives,
The observant and creatives, I sit on the beach
And the sea edifies me, the sky is palpable, the sand is eternity,
And I think, there is no place better than this.

4-8-18

THE HAUNTING

Melissa and Matt bat felt disgruntled.
They had not been invited to the forest creatures' party.
Lionel and Lisa lizard, Sarah and Sid Spider,
Mary and Martin mouse, Vick and Vanessa Vole,
Danced all day to the lark's song,
And smooched all night to the nightingale.
Melissa and Matt bat could hear all the merriment
And felt terribly ostracized.
The bats gatecrashed the party,
'Why weren't we invited?' they angrily asked.
Lionel and Lisa lizard shrugged.
Mary and Martin mouse smiled embarrassed.
Vick and Vanessa vole sidled away.
Sarah and Sid spider unconvincingly claimed,
'We didn't think it was your thing.'
Melissa and Matt bat sat at the party
And no one spoke to them.
It made them feel most self-conscious
And they hastily flew away feeling snubbed.
Hanging from their tree, Melissa and Matt bat
Began to feel resentment.
'We must devise our revenge,' they agreed.
Melissa and Matt were masters of ancient forest magic.
They opened their magnificent leather bound tome
Of antediluvian spells.
They opened the impressive book to the page

With the title, inscribed in beautiful calligraphy:

'Evoking Ghosts.'

Melissa and Matt issued a mischievous smirk,

And in their most sonorous bat voices chanted the incantation:

'Oh spirits of the arboreal realm.

Oh sprites who make corporeal unwell.

Come forth, and haunt the forest creatures.

Come forth, and make torment your feature.

Plague them. Harass them. Make their lives bad.

Reek revenge on those who made us sad.'

The bats hesitated.

The bats waited.

The night was silent…

No hint of ghoulish mental violence.

But then the grass quivered.

The grass shivered.

The blades swayed as if at play.

Then… BANG!

A refulgent flash of intense light.

There, in the misty night,

A sprite with one thing on its mind… FRIGHT!

'Who summons me from deep sleep?

Who do you want me to make weep?'

Melissa and Matt bat shook jangled nerves.

Did the forest creatures deserve

Such a wicked haunting,

Such a ghoulish taunting?

Melissa and Matt bat gathered their wits.

'It was us who summoned you oh fearful entity.'

'Why do you require my services?'

'We were not invited to the forest party.'

'What do you propose?' the glowing ghost snapped.

'The lizards, voles, mice and spiders,

We want you to haunt and torment until they express regret.'

'It will be so,' frowned the angry ghost.

So the ghost scoured the forest.

He silently floated along looking for his first victims.

Lionel lizard was leaping around

Trying to catch a butterfly for Lisa lizard with a single bound.

The chilling ghost manifested before the lizards' incredulous eyes.

'BOOH!' the ghost blurted.

'Arggghhh!' the lizards cried.

The ghost, satisfied with the scare, moved on,

Scouring the forest.

He silently floated looking along looking for his second victims.

Martin and Mary mouse were munching on some corn.

The chilling ghost manifested before the mice's incredulous eyes.

'You will regret the day you were born!' the ghost yells.

The mice jumped at such an eerie voice.

Running away was the preferred choice.

The ghost moved on, satisfied with the scare, scouring the forest.

He silently floated looking for his third victims.
Vanessa and Vick Vole were appearing from their hole.
The chilling ghost manifested before the voles' incredulous
eyes.
The ghost wailed and turned the voles' blood cold.
The ghost moved on, satisfied with the scare, scouring the
forest.
He silently floated looking for his final victims.
Sarah and Sid Spider were munching on flies.
The web glistened with mystic moonlight.
The chilling ghost manifested before the spiders' incredulous
eyes.
The spiders choked on their flies in fear
And mumbled, 'Oh, we wish we weren't here!'
The ensuing nights the ghost was relentless in his haunting,
Tenacious in his taunting.
He never gave the lizards, mice, voles and spiders
A moments peace.
'I'm giving you what you deserve!
How I enjoy getting on your nerves!' the ghost howls.
The forest creatures became fed up
And decided to meet in a secluded spot
To discuss the options they've got.
'I'm going round the bend,' mutters Sarah spider.
'I'm at my wits end,' murmured Lisa lizard.
'My nerves are in shreds,' says Martin mouse.
'I shake in my bed,' grumbles Vick vole.

'Let's call the owl. He'll know what to do.
He's the wisest in the forest. He'll get us out of this stew.'
Owl, with satellite dish ears, hears the commotion.
Glides to the stricken forest creatures in one easy motion.
Magnificent owl.
He of open eyes.
He so very wise.
Many feathered talon owl stands before the forest creatures.
'So, a ghost is bothering you,' owl nonchalantly grins.
'It's true!' the lizards, mice, voles and spiders cry.
Declares owl, 'I can remedy this for a price.'
'We will pay anything,' the forest creatures sing.
'I will name my price after I rid you of the preternatural pest,'
owl affirms.
'Anything! Anything! Just deal with that abominable ghost,'
They implore, desperate, having no sleep.
Owl spreads his marvellous wings.
The bright moon illuminates his magnificent feathers.
He flies to the centre of the forest,
Settles on a branch, and listens…
His eyes glisten with the star replete sky.
His noble head swivels 180 degrees scouring the land,
Ears sensitive to the slightest noise.
In the distance is a faint glowing.
Owls knows, it is the ghost!
The owl swoops.
Owl like a rocket silently hurtles through the midnight air

And scoops the unsuspecting ghost
In his steel grip talons.
How could owl grasp the ghost, insubstantial as light?
Owl was no ordinary bird.
Owl had been a wizard's sentinel.
Owl had learnt esoteric arts.
The ghost yelled in fear.
The ghost cried in shock.
Higher, higher, owl flew...
The ghost tried to break loose,
But owl held him like a noose.
Owl flew higher, higher, to the nearest star.
The star's fierce flame sparkled and crackled.
'Ghost, if you do not relinquish your incessant haunting,
I will drop you into the star's fierce heat.'
'But I was summoned by the bats,
And there's nothing I can do about that,' the ghost yelped.
'Oh, it can be helped,' Owl grimaced
And flew nearer the star.
The refulgent star seemed to be ravenous for the ghost
As fierce flames swirled and roared.
'Cease your haunting henceforth! This is your last chance!'
owl defiantly growled.
The ghost began sweltering so near the white hot star.
'Okay! Okay! I agree. I will return from whence I came,' the
ghost complied.
Owl, satisfied with the capitulation, let go of the ghoul,

And the stricken ghost vanished into the night.
Owl, pleased with his success, flew back to the forest creatures.
'I have done as you requested,' owl proudly announced.
'Really? Has the ghost actually gone?' they cried in unison.
'You will hear no more from him. The hauntings are over,' owl asseverated.
'Hoorah!' the forest creatures yelled in glee.
'And now for my reward,' Owl smiled.
'We had no intention of paying you,' Sid spider stated.
'Oh? But we made an agreement,' owl claimed.
'It was never in writing,' Vanessa vole smirked.
'I *will* have my reward,' owl matter-of-factly said,
And ate Lionel and Lisa lizard,
Martin and Mary mouse, Vanessa and Vick vole,
And Sarah and Sid spider.
Oh, they tried to scurry, tried to hurry,
But owl wasn't worried,
He picked them off one by one.
'What a delicious undertaking,' Owl burped.

10-8-18

ANIMATION OF THE TREES

I walk through the graveyard
And spontaneously decide to read
The book I've just brought my brother
For his birthday,
'The Complete Works of William Blake.'
And I randomly open the book
To *'The Book of Ahania'*:
I proceed to read to the graves:
'From a chariot iron-wing'd'…
The leaves in the trees above me
Begin to rustle into life.
'On spiked flames rose,'
The leaves have energy,
The trees pulse with life,
And the graves silently listen.
'Sparkles in his hair and beard.'
No one is in the spacious graveyard but me.
'His right hand burns red…'
The air is still, but the trees
Hiss as if there is strong breeze.
'His wrath as the thunder-stone…
Sons of Urizens silent burnings…'

Then I stop,
Completing the first stanza.
The buzzing of leaves suddenly cease.
The butterflies visit here
Because there is no human life:
They pollinate each gravestone.
The graves are silent.
Each inhabitant now celebrates,
Dancing in heaven,
Eternal festivities.

13-8-18

POLITICIANS

If they could vividly imagine
The destruction and misery
They cause,
There'd be no wars.

15-8-18

From grief
We grow.

15-8-18

Autonomy + Empathy = Happiness.

15-8-18

Big
Business
Busts
Butterflies.

15-8-18

Take
The easy way out
And make it
Difficult for yourself.

15-8-18

I don't measure
Success on
Material assets:
I measure
Success on
Mental facets.

15-8-18

I have nothing of material value.
I have lived in bedsits with no house of my own.
Partially because of illness my employment history is sporadic.
I owe more than I own.
But my mind has been wild and free
Searching for answers in cannabis reverie.
I speak with sparrows.
I commune with writers now asleep in the grave.
Maybe they watch…
Maybe I'll be saved.

15-8-18

If a woman allows herself
To be defined
Through a man's eyes
She can forget
Who she really is.

16-8-18

Why do I
Always find
It difficult
To stop?

I keep
On going
Always knowing
I'm going
To drop.

16-8-18

WALKING HOME FROM SUPERMARKET WITH MY FIRST NOTEBOOK.

I'm sat at Hewitt's Circus
On a dilapidated bench
On a Saturday dinner.
I've just bought this notebook,
Various writing pads,
And cheap basic pens.
I'm to start a new teaching job soon.
I plan to give the pens
To students who have forgotten theirs:
Why reward them with a good pen?

The traffic is manic.
Angry hoots:
'You're taking my lane!'
We grow,
Increasing voraciousness,
Until the planet struggles.
Will it slow, stop, reverse?
Or will the cars proliferate
Like rampant rabbits?

Vroom! Vroom!
Nigh is doom.
Zoom! Zoom!
There's no room.
Vroom! Vroom!
Danger looms.
Zoom! Zoom!
Apocalypse soon.

There's this chirpy dude,
Pony tail,
Pays with his watch:
PING!
The till girl's really impressed.
Too impressed.
She can't stop giggling.
Then I loom.
Silence…
I've bought the cheapest
Stationary in the shop.

I give her paper cash.
'I pay the old fashioned way,'
I smirk, peering into her eyes.

A house's ambience depends on the people.

State of society when the church door has:
'Thieves beware' written on it.
Pity God's wrath would not instantly
Be upon the crooks.

I sit under a rowan tree
In Old Clee church yard
On an August afternoon.
Leaves sough…
The sky is magnificent blue

With fluffy white clouds sailing by.
The gravestones are bathed in sunlight.
My shopping bag rustles with the wind.
I have bought stationary
For teaching in September.
I frequently think about
This venture now
And it fills me with purpose.
The graveyard is idyllic and peaceful.
My mind is at rest.
I am sanguine for the future.
There is a chink of light
Shining through the crack in the door.

Here ends my walk with first notebook.

18-8-18

It was bugging me,
Excuse the pun,
That I could not tell
The difference between
A dragonfly
And a damselfly.

21-8-18

Some people fail
To ethically criticize 'our side'
The same way
They ethically criticize
'The other side'.

21-8-18

Guns are horrible,
Vicious,
Spiteful implements.
You don't think so?
Then let someone
Shoot you
In the foot.

21-8-18

COMMON
EXCHANGE

The Labour Party (opposition) says there's less;
The Conservatives says there is more.

21-8-18

JUNGIAN DREAM
(PART II)

I was studying the mind, the unconscious, dream symbols.
I was espousing archetypes and theorizing on the shadow concept.
I was pursuing psychological alchemy.
I was freely interpreting religious texts, disavowing dogma,
When I was summoned before God in the sky.
I ascended to heaven and stood before his great throne.
He ran his huge fingers through his long white beard, and frowned.
'Do you know why I have brought you here?' he bellows.
His sonorous voice echoes in the clouds
As if thunder reverberated in the sky.
'No,' I meekly reply.
'I have heard of your "free-thinking".
Your latitude with hermeneutics.
I want you to display total obeisance before me.'
'Oh,' I say, 'how?'
'Genuflex your knees. Bow your head to the ground,' God roars.
I stand there for a moment, reluctant to acquiesce.
God then snarls at me and points his finger.
'Do not provoke my wrath.
I can disintegrate you with a single lightning bolt,' he yells.
I get to my knees.
I lower my head, lower, lower…
My forehead hovers 1mm above the ground.
I will not allow my forehead to touch the ground.
The 1mm gap symbolises the defiance of mankind,
The right of autonomy.
God, aware of my willful disobedience, smiles in satisfaction.

21-8-18

SNAPSHOT

It is a late August, glorious Saturday afternoon.
The benign summer sun is streaming down
Illuminating the lawn.
Whilst the daisy drinks the dew
I am sat in my dressing gown
Eating my second chocolate covered icecream lolly.
The chocolate does not crunch like on the adverts,
And the chocolate is paper thin,
But I enjoy the 'Belgian' chocolate nevertheless.
Six feet away are the conifer bushes,
And behind the bushes are four frolicking sparrows.
They take turns popping their heads out of the leaves
Assessing the situation:
Is it safe to flutter to the watering can?
Me and the sparrows have sat through this routine
All summer,
But they are still suspicious of me.

The watering can is next to the conifer bushes,
And, to my delight, one by one,
They settle on the top of the watering can
And try and drink some water.
With one eye on me,
They usually only need two quick gulps,
And they are away:
But this time the water is too shallow
For them to reach.
I go to fill it up and wait for their return,
But they are off and away exploring suburbia.
I keep meaning to take a photo of these
Resourceful little birdies,
But I decide to write about them instead.

26-8-18

A poet friend of mine said
Her daughter liked the camel drawings
I posted on social media and could she buy them.
Me thinking the art was mediocre
Set about drawing more camels,
One cubism bright orange/red camel
With cerulean sky
And refulgent yellow sand
In geometric shapes.
I took the four paintings to her house.
She gave me the money
And I threw in one of my books
Which she asked me to sign.
But by far the biggest payment
Was her daughter's glee.
This smiling girl
Proceeded to order the camel art
On the table.
She stood on a chair
And took photos of the pictures.
As I left her daughter thanked me again.
I felt elated I had pleased the child.
My artistic efforts had been vindicated
Hung on her bedroom walls.

28-8-18

People
With god complexes
Are often
Dictators.

28-8-18

Do not
Let
The bad
Silence
The good.

28-8-18

The body's instinct to live
Engenders in the mind
The belief
In an eternal soul.

28-8-18

She says sushi; I say fish fried.
I say fresh orange; she says red wine.
I say libraries; she says disco lights.
She stays awake till morning; I get early nights.
She is multi-lingual; I am a monoglot.
I'm middle aged and grey haired; she's young and very hot.

28-8-18

Before your very eyes
The skeletons will rise.
In the earth they did not budge
But bore an ancient grudge.
Do not fight them with swords
But pacify them with words.

4-9-18

I was rambling amongst the woodlands.
I was in loving communion with the forest,
Mountains and meadows.
How sweet and benign the trees sounded
In the warm dancing wind.
I was joyous at how there seemed
To be a divine life essence
In the rivers and rocks.
Then a seagull shit on my head.

4-9-18

Violence
Negates
Argument.

13-9-18

What a remarkable
Transformation
From a caterpillar
To a butterfly:
I wonder if humans
Make a similar
Metamorphosis
When they die.

13-9-18

WEELSBY WOODS

The lions in the entrance of Weelsby Woods are 100 years old, but in WW2, my dad says the lions were moved back to be replaced by sentry boxes for the Carpathian Lancers Regiment, Polish riflemen. The woods at this time had a barb wire perimeter fence because it was used as a Prisoner of War camp for German and Italian soldiers. My mam and dad were in holiday in Serrento where they got talking to a German who was imprisoned at Weelsby Woods: small world. When my dad was 7, British soldiers were on leave from guard duty and going to Cleethorpes for a drink: they asked my dad did he have any sisters, to which he replied, 'Yes.' They asked him how old were they; he replied, '4 and 3.' This greatly amused the soldiers who burst out laughing. Every Sunday there was a British military brass band marched from the camp at Weelsby Woods. After the war, the British were still stationed there, and had open days: my dad recalls climbing inside a tank.

I am now going to take you for an amble in Weelsby Woods and convey what the recreational park means to me. Recently I bought myself a little note book, intending to take it with me so I can write in situ. I usually write from the seclusion of my bedroom, but deemed it would be inspirational to write about the woods whilst I'm actually there. So this article was written as I meandered along the muddy paths that cut through the trees.

I go surging ahead: my mind in a swirl and totally neglect to see the stillness. So I sit down in the back of the woods in what we as kids called The Dead Woods. I remember summers in the woods, jumping from trees and landing in haystacks; going to the newt pond to check it out; playing football with my mates; playing cricket with my family (grandad was a big cricket fan and would sit all day watching Test Matches). I remember when I was at Havelock Comprehensive I represented the school in the Grimsby and District Cross Country Championships in Weelsby Woods. As a kid, you don't train for such an event; you've got no idea about dietary habits; just before the race you don't warm up: you just run. With 300 metres to go I had been having a personal race with a local football star from another school. All the footballing school kids in Grimsby were aware of his talent. So there we were, me and him, sprinting towards the finishing line, neck and neck. I was determined to not let him beat me. I began pulling away from him and won that little duel. As passed the finishing line, I stopped, gasping for breath, my teachers congratulated my effort (I came nowhere in the overall race). Then I threw up all over the grass. Whilst in senior school we would take motorbikes to Peak's Tunnel. We respected the code of the woods and would not fire up the engine in the more public area. I learnt how to ride a Gilera 50 Trials, and a Triumph 250 Tiger Cub Moto Cross in here whilst a kid: great fun.

As a young man I spent many years, all seasons, walking my sister's border collie in this woods: great mates me and Mist. When you walk a dog in here, fellow dog handlers will always talk to you: dog lovers have an affinity. Even without a dog, there's something about the woods that's make people more sociable: a few people today greet me as I pass. Rurality facilitates congeniality.

I am now sat by a furrowed field in the exact spot where I had a transient vision of a bright white equilateral triangle. I was not under any intoxicants and the serendipitous event left an enduring impression on me. To me, the vision signified hope, a divine intelligence in the cosmos, and consoled me much.

I can hear the humdrum cars in the distance, a continual droning hum: but here, in the woods, the silence is like another world. We are truly lucky to have Weelsby Woods, a little slice of rurality adjacent to the town. I remember a few months ago marvelling at the sight of a deer in here. I had heard others sight them, but in all my time visiting the woods, boy and man, I've never seen one. Deer are so furtive and shy so I really wished I brought my camera on that occasion. I've seen plenty of grey squirrels: if you stand quiet and still, they will do the same: and there you are, staring eye to eye for minutes with a quintessential tree dweller.

I have to say it annoys me when I see rubbish dumped in the woods. I'm now stood next to a disbanded shopping trolley, empty crisp packets and empty beer cans. Would these people leave litter strewn across their own rooms? No? So why do they think it is alright to disrespect the woods? There are litter bins provided in the park.

The trees reach up to the late summer sky. Are they trying to touch the sun, maybe escape from Gaia, Mother Earth? The soil is the trees' home, and the roots spread downwards as wide as their crowns. The invisible birds call to each other celebrating sanctuary. Bracket fungi poke out of a fallen tree looking like miniature shelves or half plates.

I have, on and off, come into the woods to shadow box. I have seen other martial artists in here practising their moves. I use the trees as imaginary opponents. You would not think I could lose! But from time to time I misjudge my range and scrape my knuckles. Beaten by a tree in round 3!

So there ends my jaunt around the woods. It's a place many would miss if it closed to the public. I have dreaded imaginings of houses being built here, or a road plastered through the middle: I think there would be an ardent public outcry if that happened. It is a place of sanctuary for me, a place where I can quietly contemplate, a refuge, an arboreal temple.

14-9-18

Some who have monsters
In their head
Terrorize others;
Some who have monsters
In their head
Edify the world.

18-9-18

Unevolved:
Owning nuclear weapons
Is like a gorilla
Beating its chest.

18-9-18

He worked fifty years for that factory.
FIFTY YEARS!
He got a little terraced house,
A little car,
But a wife and two kids.
Fifty years…
For fifty years he got a pat on the back
And a fake gold watch.

18-9-18

HORSE CHESTNUT

We're going to the countryside.
We're going to be shaking the tree.
We're going to be throwing logs at leaves,
Collect the glittering prize of conkers,
Mother Earth's produce strewn on the floor.
We frolic in the fields.
I take conkers home, a fine haul.
I violate the shiny film
And mercilessly pierce the centres with a bradawl.
I thread lace through the crumbly interior
And now I fully claim it as my own.
My conker is going to be indisputable champion.
It's going to get a conquering reputation.
It defiantly glows on the end of the string.
It's gonna rule the school playground.
My conkers gonna be unbeatable,
Just you wait and see.
I take the conker to school.
I nonchalantly swirl it round.
A kid challenges me with his puny conker.
I proudly hold up my prospective champion
For him to take a swing.
WHAM!
He smashes mine to smithereens.
I'm left holding a limp empty string.

21-9-18

SHADOW CONSCIENCE

I'm sure I've seen in the periphery
Of my vision my shadow moving
Independently of me.

Did my shadow frown
When I began irritably swearing
At the unresponsive computer?

Maybe, and for retribution,
Whilst I was in deep slumber
Pleasantly dreaming,
In the middle of the night,
It imitated a raucous alarm clock
To starkly wake me up.

'Well done!' I sarcastically say
To the dimly lit room.

In the gloomy corner,
I hear from the stillness and silence
An eerie voice whisper:
'Have patience.'

21-9-18

Sublimate
Anger
At
Travesty
Into
Calm
Eloquence.

28-9-18

I gave them water
And they thank me
With the flutter
Of their wings.

28-9-18

CRYSTALLOGRAPHY
IN IVIIX

On a dark bitter chill Prague night,
Fluffy snow falling from the black winter sky,
Johannes Kepler, wrapped in a large overcoat,
Traversed an old stone bridge that spanned a frozen river.
Johannes breathed steam as he tentatively
Perambulated over the icy ground.
A descending snowflake gently settled on the lapel of his coat
And perfectly preserved on the frozen cloth.
Johannes smiled at the immaculate symmetry.
Being an eminent scientist he felt compelled to count the sides:
One, two, three, four, five, six…
Then another dancing snowflake ensconced on his huge coat,
And he discerned, though each possessed a unique pattern,
That this frozen water from the heavens also had six sides.
He observed a number more as his coat's surface covered in snowflakes.
All the snowflakes are hexagonal, but each varies in pattern, he mused.
The hexagonal must be nature's most efficient way of building
snowflakes,
Beehives and pomegranates are also hexagonal.
It must be a fundamental construction,
As if inherent in nature a divine mathematical intelligence,
He continued to cogitate.
What an aesthetic scientific discovery, Johannes,
The inquiring scientific mind that wrote a seminal paper entitled:
'On the six cornered snowflake.'

29-9-18

CELESTIAL CRAFT

One electric winter night,
Walking amongst preternatural sky,
Crepuscular breathing trees and serpent grass rooted in my eyes,
Vegetation flowing in the marrow of my bones,
Glittering stars pressed on my mind,
Glittering stars illuminating home,
Earth, brown earth, animated moist fecund earth
Reached beyond atmospheric oxygen,
Beyond superlative still night,
Beyond momentous infinity,
Into the splendour of inexplicable dimensions,
Vibe animates network of neurons,
Tenseness of extra-terrestrial phenomena,
Palpability lodged in drumming heart,
Unearthly alien presence
From distant galactic region
In the calm still dense terra firma night,
Above wise ancient woods,
Steady pulsing lights,
Heart beat flashing lights discernibly not human,

Silent flashing lights gliding by
Meticulously observing human activity,
Undetected and unrivalled,
Capability intimidating but
Technology peacefully gliding by
Monitoring erratic human behaviour
Of an incipient civilization,
As I draw large circle, square and triangle
In the crisp yielding snow,
Universal symbols.

1-10-18

I'm tormented by her absence.
The vacancy will not leave.
She was paramount
As the oxygen I breathe.

I want to call her,
But she may not reply,
So I see a vast eternity
Without her by my side.

I know I've got to move on,
It's the grown up thing to do.
But I'm going to compare every woman
To the beauty that I knew.

9-10-18

FIRST KISS

I was 9 or 10.
I couldn't believe she was interested,
This beautiful dark haired girl.
She had a chaperone: her mate.
I began swearing a lot,
Because that's how I thought you impressed girls.
She turned round to her friend and said,
'Doesn't he swear a lot?'!
Anyway, I moved in for my first ever kiss on the lips.
It was disappointing:
Her lips were dry and I didn't know what I was doing.
All through senior school I fancied her.
She was good at netball.
We would pass in the corridor and smile at each other.
I was incapable of properly talking to girls I fancied, turned
semi-mute.
When we left school I bumped into her
In the street with her new boyfriend.
I was displeased…
I asked myself, what does he have I don't:
But now I realise:
A voice!

13-10-18

BECAUSE BEING A VIRGIN AT IVIII IS 'UNCOOL'.

It was my birthday, 18th.
I was now officially a man… ha!
I'd been drinking beer for two years.
Well, all my mates did, so why not?
The Honest Lawyer was the social hub.
Pool, beer, disco…
To celebrate, my mam and dad went away
For the weekend so I could have a party.
Old friends turned up with cans of *Worthington E,*
Vodka and whiskey.
To my delight, girls!
One I vaguely knew, but fancied.
The night wore on…
I got drunk.
I ended up with the wrong girl.
My mission was sex.
I'd been a virgin long enough.
We went upstairs on my parents' double bed.
How I fumbled and grumbled: 'I can't get it in.'
I asked her help.

With that the bedroom door swung open.
A group of party goers became an audience.
Girl, legs akimbo, my bare arse stuck in the air.
I frowned at them through the haze and they disappeared.
I made motions but didn't know if I was in!

A couple of weeks later I was playing football
On the local fields with a gang of neighbourhood kids.
She came up, watching the game.
She beckoned me over.
In my sobriety, I had totally lost interest.
'I think I am pregnant,' she said.
Alarm bells rang.
'Nope, not mine!'
I learnt later she was lying
In order to be with me.
I avoided her like the plague,
And she gradually went away.

17-10-18

HEADLESS
CHICKENS

Down in the tube station at midday
People are hurrying by.
Who's that hooded guy wearing shades?
He's warming up to play the blues on piano.
The punk rocker next to him says: 'Just play!'
So he does, boogie woogie woogie.
The punk begins in stentorian bluesy voice.
Surely the crowd hurrying by will stop.
Some stride by wearing headphones.
Hey! Are you listening to anything better than this live music?
Rush, rush, as if these two great musicians don't exist.
Hey, you're missing music,
I mean r-e-a-l music.
Hurry, hurry, scurry, scurry,
Rushing around too busy
To enjoy the good things in life.
Invisible blues player keeps on playing.
Invisible punk keeps on singing:
'Sweet home Chicago!'

17-10-18

Is there a golden thread between us
That never can be broken?
Is there more in our eyes
Than ever can be spoken?
Do you understand my sadness
When you walk away?
Is it all in my head
And there's nothing to say?

I was listening to 80s synth tonight.
The kind of music I hope you would like.
Sounds that mean so much to me.
The beat fuelled my fantasy.
I'm addicted to your glorious shine.
Woman, don't underestimate my heart.
If we danced with a smile it would be the start.

17-10-18

Millions starving
Resources shrinking
But let's keep ejaculating
Into the womb.

(Inspired by Sigue Sigue Sputnik: *Love Missile F1-11*)

17-10-18

ELEMENTARY

Battered book with appealing character.

The blurb says he is: 'The greatest fictional detective of all time.'

The image is of him trance like smoking a delicious tobacco pipe

Which facilitates his profound cogitations:

The genius mind finding impossible clues in the trivial.

The murdered man, laying there, lived in a pretty cottage.

How idyllic and peaceful.

How incongruous to the horrific events.

The corpse is clutching a fragment of paper

In his rigor mortis hand.

A clue!

Through this single scrap of paper

Holmes intends to make the impenetrable mystery

'Less obscure'.

Holmes, in confident voice, declares:

'The very hour of death is written upon the paper.'

So the hunt is on to find the rest of the telltale paper

That was violently snatched out the unsuspecting victim's hand.

18-10-18

WAR WOE

That house, there, (where?) they lived in it for forty years.
They were husband and wife, had three kids,
Many celebrations under that roof.
A bomb flattened the abode in a second.
The family now live under tarpaulin.

Don't tell me war is honourable.
I see a man tread on a land mine.
It blew him clean in two.
His legs twitched in the limp grass,
And fifteen yards away lay a lifeless torso.

Don't tell me war is honourable.
I saw a bullet explode in a woman's eye socket.
It exited her skull taking bone
The shape of a plate,
A gaping hole showing her raw brain.

Don't tell me war is romantic.
I see a child with arms blown away.
Screams pervade the rubble street.
Now growing up with a life of trauma.

Don't tell me war is chivalrous.
The bullets indiscriminately spray
Never looking deep into the eyes of the bloody recipient.
Death and destruction,
Hate and anger,
Fear and loss,
Grim reaper grins in satisfaction.

The artery severed, never
To be repaired.
The blood squirted like
A full on tap.
The man screamed in dire agony,
'Tell my family I love them.'
He would never be going back,
Internal bleeding would see to that.

You cheered as they went away.
You waved your patriotic flags.
But now you welcome their return with tears,
Hidden in body bags.

26-10-18

HOPE

The four year old girl
Clutching a dishevelled teddy
Is skipping along the aisles of library books.
Her little hand runs along each spine
Like a stick along railings.
Her uninhibited smile is palpable.
Her mother will read to her this evening
As she is tucked up in bed.
Where will the book take you, little girl?
To a magical land made of sweets,
Or a land of fairies and unicorns
Where the evil sorcerer tries to rule the land,
But good prevails over evil, like all good endings?
Will the fairies dance and sing
And cast spells to make flowers bloom?
Will the unicorns soar in the sky
Spreading benevolence over fairy land?
Will the words on the page make you smile
And induce pleasant dreams in your deep slumber?
Will your imagination be fuelled
As images of fairy land permeates your active mind?
Will you learn new words like: fabulous, marvellous and wonderful?

The inherent morality in you will be satisfied
When the fairies restore the natural order.
You will look at books in wonder
And develop a lifelong reading habit.
As you grow you will become eloquent
And articulate and explore new ideas.
You will express yourself effectively
And the contentment of the victorious fairies
Will be a firm foundation in your life.

26-10-18

Grosswatch the ogre had a cold dark soul,
As dark as any hole.
And what he loathed the most,
From any girl or boy,
Was to see their joy.
One day he saw two children at play.
They were laughing with glee and looked so happy.
They played ball and skipped down the street.
Grosswatch the ogre hoped they would trip their feet.
He gnarled and snarled.
Their laughter was like poison to his ears.
He grimaced and frowned.
These two children's joy was getting him down.
He groaned, 'I hate to see them happy.'
Then it was time for tea,
So the children went into their house.
Grosswatch the ogre said, 'I'm going to make them pay
For all the appalling happiness today.'
So he devised a plan.
Tonight he would scare the two children awake
By putting in their bedroom a slithery snake.
Night came and he crawled up a ladder
To their bedroom window.

'In you go,' he sneered to the snake.
The children were sound asleep
Having pleasant dreams about a house
Made of chocolate cake.
In slithered the snake towards their beds.
Closer, closer, closer it slithered
Until it reached their heads.
Grosswatch the ogre gave an evil smirk
As he peered through the window.
'The snake will teach you not to be happy,' he said.
But the snake saw the two sleeping children's smile
And it warmed his cold reptilian heart.
He gently kissed the children on their foreheads,
And then attacked Grosswatch the ogre for his evil plan.
Grosswatch the ogre couldn't have been sadder:
He slipped and fell off his ladder.
He yelped down the street dragging his huge feet.
Grosswatch the ogre? He never changed.
He still has a cold dark soul,
Dark as any hole.

26-10-18

The sun leapt from out the ground
Illuminating the grassy rolling hills.
The trees like sentinels all in a row
Stand contemplative and calmly still.
The fluffy sparrows sat along the hedge
Greet the refulgent orange dawn.
After sweet dreams I draw the curtains open
To welcome the congenial gentle morn.
What the day will bring is mainly down to me.
A positive attitude means that I will be happy.

28-10-18

I walk amongst tombs that perceive.
Epitaphs of love and sweet ever lastings.
The dense stillness is observing my heart.
Seagulls shit wherever they choose,
For only food is sacred in a sea bird's soul.
Nothing's sacred in the capitalist's greed:
Music, art, literature cynically used
To sell the polluting car.
The squirrel, pensive, squats on a grave
Trying to comprehend the human smile.
Plastic roses on the graves not as beautiful
As reality but far more durable.
The stone angel's wing is clipped,
But she still signifies our grand aspirations.

4-11-18

He was a deluded lad.
At pugilism not too bad.
He was the cockiest in the gym.
Thought he'd always win.
No one told him he had no chin.
'I'm gonna win a title.
Success for me is vital.
All I gotta do is train.
I got what it takes.'
So he would dance around the heavy bag
Trying to be Muhammad Ali.
Sometimes his shoulders would sag,
But he thought we couldn't see.
He would train till all his energy had gone,
But as yet he'd had no fights, not one.
Then the big night came.
With his first fight he thought of fame.
'I'm gonna win in three,
A stunning victory.
I refuse to lose!'
He stepped into the ring.
Thought he'd be king.
But what he didn't see,
Was his opponent was mean.
His opponent was hungry and lean.
His opponent was fierce and keen.
The bell sounded and here we go.
The deluded lad was light on his toes.
He danced around the ring like Fred Astaire.
But pretty soon he wishes he wasn't there.
He threw a sloppy punch,

Hi opponent easily slipped it and countered with a powerful straight right.
Deluded lad's nose instantly broke, on his blood he choked.
Now deluded lad realised he was in a fight.
All his cockiness, his self-assuredness, his confidence,
Drained out the soles of his feet.
His opponent saw the change in demeanour,
Made him keener.
He moved in for the kill.
The crowd felt a thrill, cheered for blood.
Deluded lad turned to rubber.
Short right hook to the ribs,
Short left hook to the temple,
Devastating screw-shot to the chin,
And deluded lad was ready to give in.
Straight right to the broken nose,
Over deluded lad goes.
He's on his knees totally exposed.
The ref doesn't intervene in time,
Solid upper cut to the head,
And deluded lad lays there half dead.
Deluded lad, where oh where are you now?
You ain't in the gym boasting about a win.
You sit in your wheel chair
Drinking coffee through a straw
Watching daytime TV.
You don't even think of what might have been.
You do now realise how tough boxing really is.
It is a sport you'll never miss.

4-11-18

ATTITUDE

I am 'super sub.'
On the pitch I am hub.
I'm someone my team mates can trust.
By the power of my will
I've developed my skills.
Manager brings me on when we are losing.
I don't mind the tackles and the bruising.
I've scored a spectacular 20 yard volley,
Loyal supporters went home feeling jolly.
Once I scored two goals in the last 15 minutes:
For a promotion place, it meant we were still in it.
I have an instinct for being in the right place;
Like a phantom I glide into space.
I pass the long ball like Glen Hoddle;
I dribble the ball like Chris Waddle;
I have as much passion as Paul Gascoigne.

I can sprint turn 180 degrees on a coin.
Grimsby Town manager, Bill Shankly, said,
'Aim for the sky and you'll reach the ceiling.
Aim for the ceiling and you'll stay on the floor.'
I've got the drive and determination to always score.
I don't get down if we lose:
There's always next match to prove
To the manager and the fans
That Town give it all, every man.
I'm a goal poacher.
A bit of a joker.
I never give up hope.
Always able to cope.
Tenacious until victorious.

10-11-18

MARC CHAGALL

At your birth fire leapt into the sky,
Flames flickered in the province.
You lay there, still, motionless, moribund.
They needled you into life.
Suddenly a burst from your baby lungs.
Your anguished cry pervaded the Russian village.
Marc lives!
You grew in abject poverty rooted in sadness.
But then you picked up the paint brush!
It mystically glistened in your seven fingered hand.
With dashing strokes earth and sky merged.
Play on! Play on! Green Violinist
As Marc unfettered dances on your nose.
Peer into the mirror, gaze into genius.
Frown at Classical statues, rigid and cold.
Your academy is the bustling streets,
People divine, mystical landscapes.

Your innovative eyes transform and beautify.
Bella, Bella, your beautiful wife
Ethereally manifests sanctifying love.
Plunge your brush into unadulterated colour
And let paint freely fly!
Marc, gleefully dance on the ceiling,
Glide through the sky.
Your replete heart is the enchanted Firebird
Magically transforming sorrow to joy.
Ineffable art beyond corporeal realm.
Glowing windows painted with light.
Process the desert of shoes.
Reach beyond the horizons
And cradle the universe.

11-11-18

If individuality causes hostility
What does it say about society?

16-11-18

The power
Of poetry
To instill puissance
In a person.

16-11-18

For the sake of all nations
Rise above indoctrination.

16-11-18

Unchallenged
Authority
Leads
To tyranny.

16-11-18

ABANDONED HOPE

I never sleep, hence never dream.
I am a lost soul
Consigned to mope in hell for eternity.
I am reduced to a vague grey shadow.
My despondency, my depression,
My desperation knows no bounds.
As I passed through hell's gates
I had hope I would escape,
But, 'Abandon all hope ye who enter.'
Over the aeons I have reluctantly
Accepted my horrid fate.
Here, in this murky gloom,
It is always winter, always chill,
With no colour but grey.
The bitter cold mist
Engulfs me like a fist.
How I regret my behaviour on earth.
This interminable time in desolate solitude
Has given me time to reflect.

I was misanthropic,
Cynical of all mankind.
I criticized all I encountered.
I felt contempt and mocked everyone.
I thought I could act with impunity,
Do as I pleased without consequences.
I exploited the vulnerable,
Took advantage of the weak.
But my behaviour did not go unheeded.
Divine retribution was upon me at death.
The cosmic committee see all!
I now wander aimlessly in this bleak
World of doomed shadows,
Burdened with profound regret.

16-11-18

PHOENIX CHIMP (FIRST VERSION)

The alpha male chimp was attacked by a gang of rival male chimps and they tore chunks out of him and bit off his finger and he was laying there moribund and some females came and licked his wounds but then the troop left him for dead and went to search for water and he lay there vulnerable to predators and after a few days he stirred and gorged on plants and ants and then limped off to find the troop and he found them and a wannabe alpha male approached him and challenged for leadership but this weak and maimed chimp began posturing and snarling showing his teeth and he intimidated the stronger male with his cunning toughness and bravery and before long he re-established himself as leader and won the golden prize of mating rights and had a baby male chimp to continue his eminent line.

20-11-18

The world couldn't contain him
So the inflexible world slain him
Shamanic poet
Indian dancer
Glider into alternative dimensions
Wild man of rock
Intelligent man of words
Provoker
Lover
Smoker
Brother
Riler of apathy
Primeval screamer supplicate the sleepers
We don't want your world of uniforms
And standing to attention
We wanna step into alternative dimensions
Feeling alive
Living in the parameters with immaculate perception
We ain't gonna take this
Shake off chains of conformity
And set ourselves free
Be who we want to be
Ray's magic fingers summon our ancestors on keyboard
Robby's screeching guitar tap into my reptilian soul
John play that tribal beat
The shaman is about to leap
See him dance in a trance on atavistic feet
Essential self
Primal expression
Spiritual lesson
Once cleansed

24-11-18

LAST NIGHT'S DREAM:

I was climbing to the top.
I didn't stop.
I was going till I dropped.
Each step a life time's effort.
Clambering up the rock.
On and on to the top.
No thought of stopping.
Heavy arms nearly dropping.
Climbing up the rock.
Then I reached the top.
A panoramic view.
Scenes anew
As far as my eyes can see.
A land sticky.
Expansive oil fields.
Everywhere black shiny gooey oil.
All that toil just to see
Expansive sticky oil fields.

27-11-18

Proud lion
Swaggering lion
Roaming the plains of Africa
Not a care in the world
Don't push me, I bite
I fear nothing
I'm so fierce
I'm so strong
I got teeth
I got claws
Crazy pack of giggling hyenas
Famished loons surround lion
Bite his hind quarters
Take it in turns to bite him
He occasionally grasps one
Mauls it
But it writhes free
20 fanatical crazy hyenas
Barking, howling, laughing, biting
Ha ha ha we're going to eat you alive
The lion's getting tired
He looks scared

The predator becomes the prey
The instinct to survive is strong
They harass him
Circle him
Bite him
Taunt him
He growls but fear is in his eyes
Crazy loony hyenas laughing biting
In the distance a growl
The lion takes hope
It is his cousin, a fellow proud fierce lion
His cousin strolls into the centre of the hyenas
Now it's two lions side by side
Two lions are a different prospect
The hyenas quickly assess the situation
And soon slink off
The two lions greet each other
Rub heads
Pleased to see each other
Two lions so much mightier than one

27-11-18

The extra-terrestrials infiltrate every TV on earth...

INAUGURAL
SPEECH

We've been meticulously observing your earth for hundreds of years. We know in the history of the human race there has never been world peace. Your incessant wars are notorious throughout the universe. You are relentlessly motivated by insatiable greed, pride, hate and anger. You absurdly estimate the value of all things by what you call money. In 1945 we extra-terrestrials incredulously witnessed Hiroshima and Nagasaki. And now a handful of your countries have the technology to destroy beautiful planet earth. Indeed, your technology has advanced far quicker than your ethics. We have watched your fossil fuel machines gradually erode the ozone layer and increase climate temperatures. Your systematic deforestation has to be immediately curtailed. Your exponential population proliferation has to be mitigated. You are two generations away from complete annihilation. We could not sit back as impartial observers any longer. We have unanimously decided to comprehensively intervene before it is too late. We have, with the use of cosmic rectification waves, decommissioned all your weapons. Nuclear weapons are now rendered harmless.

Not even a bullet can be fired. We have also disabled all fossil fuel engines. We are replacing them with sustainable clean energy sources designed by our advanced races. We are even intervening with your economy to ensure a more equitable distribution of wealth. Because planet earth is incapable of governing itself, we, the extra-terrestrials, are taking over. We did not take the decision lightly. Our prime directive had stated non-interference with alien cultures, but we had to do it in order to ensure the survival of the human race.

1-12-18

HERE AND NOW

I am now going to talk about the Here and Now. The true Now is always here and past Nows are inevitably superseded by the present Now. There are infinite past Nows but only one present Now. I know the past Nows are not strictly Nows but I'll call them Now for now. They irrefutably used to be Nows. Past Nows are negated to past memories. Our finite minds cannot recall the comprehensive concatenation of past Nows but the present Now is vivid. The past Nows change with our experiences and we colour them with subjectivity but the present now is incontrovertible, though even that is individually perceived. This Now for me is different to this Now for you even though we are both here, so arguably there are an infinite number of Nows now. Can you see how as I've stood here talking about Nows now how I've changed my stance on the present Now from one absolute present Now to a multitude of Nows? I will now talk about the Here. The Here is always here. There is only one Here, everything else is elsewhere. The Here is quintessential existence. Let us now embrace the Here whilst sometimes pondering what it's like over there. Thank you for being Here in the Now. Now I'm going to get out of Here!

9-12-18

JUNGIAN INFLUENCE

The guardians of sentience continually comprehensively observe.
I plunder my voracious mind for a certain sign
Of transcendent manna divine.
I supplicate the numinous for my spiritual guide.
Introversion connects to magnificent extraneous.
Submerging through the unconscious
To the glorious archetypal foundation
Increases consciousness and awareness.
Ancient immutable symbols augment cosmic soul.
Embrace optimism in the refulgent equilateral triangle.
Gaze in universal eyes that shine cultivated love.
Through individuality we locate commonality.
Satisfying congruity with patience and understanding.
Listen to the musicians' wisdom musing on memorable magic.
Nostalgia and nature facilitate the essential groove.
Believe in the light and the human race will survive.
Master the shadow and refute inimical influential credibility.
Disavow insatiable ostensible materiality.
Satisfy spirituality by seeking fulfilling objectives.
Lapse into prejudice and ineluctable division persists.
Do not project unacknowledged inadequacies on the unsuspecting.
Cynicism induces vehement indelible hostility.
If we all push exhaustion is inevitable.
If we harmonize we can realize the Utopian dream.
Like honey in coffee gently take her warm hand.
Her smile is the beacon we must follow.

13-12-18

LLANBEDROGOCH

Below a silent blue sky with calm clouds sailing by,
At a tranquil picturesque rural site,
The shimmering grass whispering ancient secrets,
Lying motionless for generations amongst the cold stone,
Is the contorted skeletal remains of a young man.
He has silently laid there forgotten for 1200 years.
His sardonic grin belies the abrupt violent death.
He lays contorted, arms behind his back.
He has been bound, slain, and unceremoniously
Slung in a shallow grave and covered by stone,
Buried without ritual merely to prevent animals eating the corpse.
There's no indicator in the bones of incision,
But soft tissue, veins and arteries, could have been brutally sliced.
I read the book, *Blood of the Vikings*, further on,
Women and children also excavated in this prominent archaeological dig,
Laying forlorn in a similar manner.
My father told me when I was a child
I had Viking blood seething through my veins.
My greatgrandad, Ragnovild Vagnus Nilsen, was born in Norway.
He was awarded a medal for valour presented by the Dutch Queen.
He single handedly took a rowing boat
Into stormy seas to save a stricken man,
But alas the man was already dead.

My greatgreatgrandad was a whaler, salty sea dog.
(I'm all for protecting whales, but then was a different era.)
My greatgrandad was a skipper on the Seine Netters,
Small Scandinavian fishing boats.
His family owned forests outside of Oslo,
But he gave up his inheritance when he met a Grimsby girl,
Married her, settled here and became a lumper on Grimsby
docks
Like many former fishermen.
In my uninformed naiveté, I was proud of Viking ferocity,
The indomitable warrior reputation,
But I look at the photograph of this pitiful skeleton,
Hands bound behind his back in a shallow grave,
Dying a violent premature death,
The evidence of Viking ruthlessness,
And I rethink my bias and pride.

16-12-18

So, I have another mouse in my box bedroom,
And don't it scurry like a rocket when it sees me!
But my presence does not deter it scavenging for food.
It starts roaming round the bedroom like I'm not there.
I reluctantly set two traps with blobs of cheese.
The mouse gently takes the cheese and does not activate the trap.
I regrettably reset the traps with chocolate.
The mouse with dexterity again takes the bait and the trap doesn't go off.
I reset the trap using smaller bait.
I lay in the night conscious of a little furry creature
Scurrying around the carpet.
In the dark: SNAP!
I switch the bedroom light on.
There, tail and hind legs twitching, is the little brown mouse.
I pick the trap up: the little creature is limp and dead, body sags.
I leave the mouse in the trap and go back to bed.
It's unpleasant laying there with death in the room.
In the morning I go to the trap: the mouse is now stiff as a board.
Only a few hours and rigor mortis coldly creeps in.
It's lantern eyes now faded.
Sorry, little mouse, but you running around the house is unsanitary.
You came in from the winter's cold
To meet a sudden violent death neck breaking instantly.
You would have nibbled my books,
Maybe electric cables,
Defecated,
Bred an infestation.
Outside you're fine, run free;
But inside, you had to be exterminated.
Sorry.

23-12-18

Regarding history, is epistemological hermeneutics
always inevitably subjective?

23-12-18

Somewhere in deep sweltering Africa,
And this is sadly true,
There is a young albino woman.
She is almost blind, but struggles on with life,
Makes the best of what she has,
Which is very little.
There is a belief by a credulous few in Africa
That an albino's hands have magic healing properties.
So these two stupid fuck wits broke into her humble home
And cut her hands off,
Stole them to sell…
And so later, there she is, blind,
Waves her two stumps and smiles for the tv camera.
And I think, what ignorance!
What audacity!
What barbarism!
How incredible that people sink so low
To hatchet off those two precious hands
For a small amount of cash.

23-12-18

Christmas Eve
And winter is here.
Some say it is drear,
But I say there's beauty
Anytime of the year.
The robin sings song.
There's snow on the lawn.
I drink lots of tea
To keep me warm.
I'm thankful to wake
On this frosty morn.

24-12-18

Timidity can get you killed;
Fearlessness can too:
It's good to walk the middle way,
Just like Aristotle says.

28-12-18

I have stood at the bus stop
Through sun, rain and snow.
I have stood silent with strangers
I may like to know.
Mid-afternoon, school comes to a close,
Time for children to let off steam,
For all day behind tables they have been.
I hope all their futures
Are much like their dreams.
I went to Havelock from 1975.
Even now some of my dreams are still alive.
We look down Carr Lane for the bus to arrive.
Time is precious as we stand here and wait.
We hope the bus will not be too late.
We have places to go and things to complete.
I smile seeing the bus driving up the street.
In my hand is the bus fare.
I hop on board and forget my cares.
Thank you for reading my little poem.
I wish you all a safe journey home.

28-12-18

On Christmas day I walked past an old lady
Sat on a chair in her front garden,
And she was immersed in her iphone.
I wanted to inquire of her well-being,
Just to wish her merry Christmas,
But I just looked and went silently by.
I mildly chastised myself.
I wondered if she was lonely.
Why else would she be sat on her own
In the front garden?
I hope her family and friends visit today.

28-12-18

Perpetual antediluvian glow
Of immutable sacred soul
In quest of hospitable home
And augmentation of cosmic spirituality
Facilitated by supplicating assurance
From guardians of sentient eternity
Prophesying momentous moment
Of extricating decrepit skin
As immortal youth refulgent shines
Potent benevolent love within.

28-12-18

I am a crumbly brown brick.
I am of the earth and I flourish in the sun.
I smell deceptively delightful.
I look innocuous enough,
But I contain intense joy,
Profound introspection,
And abject paranoia.
I can bring people together,
They laugh and talk nonsense,
Amnesia is hilarious,
The familiar a fascination…
But the corrupt world can impede,
Thoughts of impending doom,
Persecution and misconception,
Panic can pervade and manic delusion.
If you try me I may coax you
Into always being my friend.
You will depend on me.
I will replace everyone in your life.
You will vanish into the shadows.
You will dissipate into the gloom.
I sit, a crumbly brown brick,
Looking innocuous:
Try me at your peril!

29-12-18

KILKENNY IVIII III V

Magnificent white horses panting and pulling
A prosperous young fop in a gleaming stagecoach.
He is sat in elegant attire,
Gold diamond rings twinkling in the frosty morning sun,
Complaining about the weather and the state of his business.
He voraciously munches on gooseberries,
Greedily smacking his rubber lips,
Gooseberry juice dripping from his multiple chins,
As he reverberantly belches from his ample gut.
He nonchalantly spits the gooseberry skins
Out of the stage coach window
And the chewed skins splatter onto the muddy track.

The wheels of the coach spit mud
On a desperate young mother dressed in hessian rags
Carrying a hungry screaming baby.
The destitute mother espies the gooseberry skins
Ejected from the stage coach window into the cold dank mud.
She carefully picks up each gooseberry skin
And sadly peers at the flaccid husks.
She then lovingly places one into the baby's mouth,
Who begins gratefully chewing on the cast off fruit skin.
It assuages the baby's emptiness
And momentarily ceases to sob.

3-1-19

The glittering universe danced on her precious skin
As her captivating song summoned sleeping spirits,
Who, fascinated, located where the charming melody emanated from.
The ancient entities were wholly satisfied.
Her resonating eyes hypnotized the night.
Her panacea smile dissipated all concerns.

I will fashion myself into a being she will deem agreeable.
I have eternity to surmount the gulf and create connection.
I am a sleeping prince amongst a forest of thorns.
I must participate in a world of facades and be ready for epiphany.
Dance on lovely woman, sing your heart-felt song.
Know I appreciate your soul's decanting into my purged mind.
My stalwart heart will endure the interminable passage of time.
My granite foundation will always remain.
I will stand alone and be self-contained.
I tolerate disappointment as the years trickle by.
I will cultivate purpose until I age and die.

8-1-19

The world
Doesn't change
Because of realists:
The world
Changes
Because of idealists.

8-1-19

Poetry is arguably the cream of any language.

Even colloquialism can be an effective mode of expression in a sincere poem.

Poetry helped saved my life, maybe literally!

As I lay in bed, severely ill, at certain times suicidal, I began writing poetry.

All my angst, my despair, my misery, I vented onto the paper.

Oh, those early poems probably weren't that good.

Poor syntax perhaps.

But it contributed in assuaging my anguish.

Nevertheless, I burnt all those early poems.

I was worried they would get into the wrong hands.

My manic craziness exposed.

The unprincipled exploit vulnerability.

I remember the very first poetry book I bought, I was about 29.

At first I didn't understand a single poem.

Frustrated, I thought about returning the book:

But I persevered and was rewarded with a beautiful new language.

Eventually I understood every poem in the book.

It was a great sense of achievement and satisfaction for me.

Fast forward to the vicinity of the present.

Poetry has enabled me to meet people like you.

Poetry has given me a voice.

Poetry has raised my self-esteem and helped me overcome social anxiety.

Poetry has facilitated in psychologically healing me.

Poetry has greatly consoled me.

In poetry nothing is ordinary.

Poetry bridges gaps and connects people.

I read the minds of others and know I'm not alone.

I hear the heart and soul of people like you.

I cannot think of my life without poetry now.

I look forward to the future exploring new poems,

Re-reading familiar poems and increasing comprehension.

Dead poets are like old friends, they live on through the printed word.

I look forward to attending more poetry gatherings,

Trying out new poems on you.

I love the challenge of discovering new ideas for poems.

So here's to poets alive and dead,

You have played a crucial part in my life.

THANK YOU!

8-1-19

PHOENIX CHIMP
(APEX APE)
(SECOND VERSION)

The alpha male chimp was attacked by a gang of rival male
chimps…
They tore chunks out of him and bit off his finger…
He was laying there at the point of death…
Some females came and licked his wounds
But then the troop left him for dead and went to search for
water…
He lay there vulnerable to predators…
After a few days he stirred…
He gorged on plants and ants and partially recovered…
He then limped off to find the troop…
He found them and a wannabe alpha male approached him,
Challenged for leadership…
But this weak and maimed chimp began posturing
And snarling showing his teeth…
He intimidated the stronger male
With his cunning toughness and bravery…
Before long he re-established himself as leader,
Won the golden prize of mating rights,
Had a baby male chimp to continue his eminent line…

11-1-19

ANTITHETICAL EXISTENCE

I was living in the city of Norwich.

I had been teaching at a Secondary School there.

On my first morning I was calmly sat in the staffroom, feeling slightly anxious.

Suddenly a man burst in, looked over to me and began glaring and scowling.

He marched over and curtly introduced himself as my mentor.

From that moment on he tried to assert his authority at every opportunity.

He systematically negatively criticized every aspect of my teaching practise.

His totalitarian approach allowed no compromise.

Once he growled, 'You WILL do as I say.'

I became popular with my students: this irked him further.

Then out of the blue, he issued an edict

In the form of two full A4 sheets basically stating my abject 'incompetence,'

Not a single positive comment.

So far I was passively accepting his reign of terror,

But that was enough for me: I had nothing to lose.

I responded with heated indignation and railed at the flagrant travesty,

Clearly stating he was abusing his authority and he was a bully.

He was flabbergasted and it just gave him more ammunition.

I was reprimanded by the headmaster, who had a conspicuous gavel on his table:

The head willfully ignored all my protestations.

I stuck it for nearly an academic year.

On my last day I stood outside the school with a wry smile,
Feeling ambivalent, glad to see the back of him,
But I would miss the kids.

It is glorious summer solstice in Norwich.
I am now free from institutionalized conformity.
No more straitjacket white shirt and tie.
I am stood in the back garden of the house I lodge in.
The smiling sun is beating down.
I want to celebrate the summer solstice so I strip naked.
My bare feet caress the luscious grass.
I am rooted in the ancient soil,
Profound spiritual connection with Mother Earth.
I begin to dance: I writhe, I gyrate.
I nakedly dance laughing care free.
It starts to rain, gentle warm summer rain splashes on my naked skin.
Next to me, my companions, red flushed rose bushes.
The rain, precious jewels, lovingly kiss rose petals.
The petals shimmer and sparkle in the refulgent sun,
Droplets of rain splash upon stunning red beauty.
The roses laugh merrily at my insouciant dancing.
I laugh and sing and whirl in the summer rain.
I am sky dancing with the sacred light.
I am free. I AM FREE!

12-1-19

DIOGENES

He was the fierce dog-man wearing God's sagacious apparel.
He modestly lived in an old wooden barrel.
He begged money from statues to grow accustomed to refusal.
He was deeply cynical of mankind after diligent perusal.
He despaired at all the malleable sheep,
But he never lost any comforting sleep.
He was a Stoic of the highest order,
Some say on the border of unrestrained madness.
Alexander the Great said: 'I'll give you anything you want.'
He replied: 'Stop blocking the sun.'
I can only imagine Alexander saw the irresistible fun
In this eccentric dishevelled old gentleman.
He walked around in the day with a lamp.
When asked why, he replied: 'I'm looking for a man.'
His measure of a human being
Was criteria others were apparently not seeing.
He believed most fell short;
They were inauthentic and easily bought.
Society's limited conventions easily distort.
He would not adhere to the blatant act.
He spoke plain and matter-of-fact.
In the everyday he always saw valuable treasures,
Extolling all the simple pleasures.
An old man with intense staring eyes.
Many conversed with him: heterodox wise.

23-1-19

INELUCTABLE

The glorious full moon was shining almost as bright as the sun.

I found myself in a forest of magical silhouettes.

My feet were planted in the soil; my head pervading the sky.

I had affinity with the roots of trees sucking moisture from the earth;

I was intimate with the stars, each quintessence of light.

A fox boldly approached me, trusting, as if I was a companion.

I felt a sensation on my shoe, and there a robin perched.

Then, a sonorous voice from the shadows proclaimed, 'It is time!'

I anxiously peered into the darkness, trying to ascertain what lunar creature this was.

The majestic voice continued, 'You are to be initiated into the sacred rites of the cosmos.'

As I could not descry any corporeal form, I felt cynical and hesitant.

'I do not wish it,' I nervously murmured.

'You have been chosen by the preternatural realm. We have been assessing your suitability from birth. We deem you are now ready,' the voice declared.

'What does it entail?' I inquired.

'Open your heart. Open your mind. Be receptive to the powers of immutable nature,' the voice asseverated.

At once I felt inadequate and fear overwhelmed me.

My panic broke the spell and I began to run.

I ran through the forest like a stricken deer.

My only aim was to reach the outskirts of the town.

I ran and ran and never looked back.

Behind me I heard a pitiable howl of lament,

As if the forest was expressing a profound disappointment.

The forest's sorrow made me uncontrollably weep.

The huge night sky pervaded my mind.

I had visions of the sleeping forest creatures' dreams.

My awareness increased: my soul augmented.

Galaxies swirled in my brain.

I saw myself in everything.

The shadow creature's prophecy had come true.

The initiation was complete.

I was now a sorcerer, a guardian of the earth.

I was privy to the sacred mysteries.

My mission was to make evil look ridiculous.

28-1-19

YACHT CLUB
(HUMBERSTONE
FITTIES)

I was gliding among razor grass sand dunes
Stretching towards a blanket of louring grey.
The fanged frozen wind nibbles my ungloved hands.
Fellow poets, unrecognizably cocooned in hoods,
What words are formulating on this winter afternoon?
Bait diggers systematically tug reluctant lug worm
From their cozy subterranean dens.
Grey silent sea forts, a relic of atrocious war,
Calmly stand sentinel over the barren coast.
Behind me, sustainable energy,
Giant revolving fans powering steaming kettles.
Seagulls, sailors of the sharp air,
Glide forever vigilant for nourishment.
Dogs merrily bound on vast flat sand,
Each time like their first visit.
Winter's breath scatter sand grains
Racing past leaping dogs.

Lego freighters in the refrigerated haze
About to dock after long voyages
To unload the latest model 4 by 4,
Each ship a metal island of disciplined crew,
The tiny lighthouse a reminder we care for their safety.
The relentless frothy tide churns
An imposing panoply of marching foam.
Sand and sea deceptively innocuous,
Do not let the mesmeric shushing
Lull you into complacency,
Disaster awaits the unsuspecting.
Solitary spots of rain tap on my hood,
Messengers from the domed firmament.
A beached yacht's awnings melodically flap
Waking me from reverie.
Images of steaming hot chocolate
Now tantalize my taste buds.
Time to head indoors and mingle with the poets.

1-2-19

SPECIAL SOUL

There is summer sky in your warm eyes.
I see sanctuary in your candid smile.
You are gentle but passionate.
You are talented and considerate.
Your nature-connection cultivates spirituality.
With everyone you meet there's always amicability.
I always feel enlivened in your presence.
You are the closest I can be to heaven.
I have no desire to bind you.
My only desire was to find you.

1-2-19

I wanna tell you
What music means to me.
I was born in 1963,
When The Beatles
Started making history.

25-2-19

The big cat
Cannot get fat
Because it's losing
Natural habitat.

25-2-19

Sat in the back row.
3d glasses over normal glasses.
Smear upon smear.
Speakers booming.
I actually put fingers in ears.
Movie appears.
Clever, kind of charming in places…
FLASH, BANG, WHALLOP,
ZOOM, BOOM, VROOM,
ACTION, ACTION, ACTION,
SMACK, CRACK, FLASH,
DAZZLE, SPEED, ERRATIC…
Sensory overload,
Head buzzing,
Want to look away
But have paid.
Excessive stimulation
Eventually dulling perception
Evolutionary regression
Zombiefication…

Outside cinema.
Shadows and chill.
Joggers and walkers.
I eat fish and chips
From a Styrofoam tray.
I walk onto the beach.
Soft sand acquiesces.
The silent sea surges
Along the beach.
I look at the still moon.
My senses replete
As the sea nibbles
My heels.
A girl on the pier
Holds up inflatable
Numbers for a photograph.
She's either 16, 19, 61 or 91!
She is young,
A future of virtual reality.

25-2-19

A corner stone
Of every functioning
Democracy
Is an accessible
Comprehensive
Free public library.

25-2-19

She thinks
Success
Is an
Expensive
Dress.

25-2-19

JOY DIVISION

Everything topples when there's no room.
Stuck in a concrete cancer,
Nothing but factory fodder,
No wonder we were beer boys.
In a blue room I see serene sky
Whilst chaos insists it exists.
I escape to the electric circus
And pogo in a punk club.
Wherever I go it's no go.
They won't do it so I'll do it myself.
I can't relate to their waiting.
There's happy accidents in a box of words.
Their frenzied explosion rebels against television.
Isolation is a way of life.
Keeping on keeping on with venomous anger.
We play in the shadows
As the room with no window waits.
The sewers crumble
As underground resistance ascends.
My churning stomach reminds me
We live in digital heaven.
There is a bleak bridge to chilling eyes.
The inane laughing lunatic
Tells me unknown pleasures await in the wave pattern.
I searched the city and found no fun.

To penetrate the darkness I was too young.
The colony of dead souls kill my dreams.
Fragility and strength
Recites metaphorical lacerations.
Cut the strings of the twitching puppet.
I love her and I love her and I love her.
We are nothing in isolation;
We are everything in solitude.
By the atrocity exhibition I am mesmerized.
Step inside watch him writhe.
Horrors cannot be denied.
He conceals his pain
As the darkness is revealed.
Let's take a short-cut through the graveyard.
He was committed to the act.
In his memory play the albums back to back.
There is only room for the tomb.
Carry on and create a New Order.
There's always new tunes.
Let's leave no one abandoned.
If I had one minute remaining, what would you say?
Would you look away?

25-2-19

TELEPHONE
I IX VIII VII

The phone in the hall summons me.
I phone her. I wanna hear my girl.
Her mam answers. I ask for Trix.
Her mam, in cold indifference,
No sign of usual friendliness, says,
'I'll get her for you.'
Trix answers. 'Yes,' was all she said.
No happy *hi*, just a flat monotone *yes*.
'What's wrong?' I earnestly ask.
'You slept with Sue last night.'
I couldn't believe she knew, and so soon too.
I couldn't deny it. My fiancée.
My girlfriend for nearly five years.
The pit of my stomach churned.
Already I could feel I was losing her.
Lost her.
She had already forgiven my past indiscretions
On the agreement I would not repeat them,
But this was the final straw.
'Er, I was drunk… I, I… How do you know?'
'She told me first thing this morning.'
Sue, the bitch, couldn't wait to spill the beans:
She just wanted to split me and Trix up.
'I'm sorry… It meant nothing… I, I…'
The *I* disappeared into resignation.
I knew this was it. I'd blown it.
She put the phone down.

Hearing the clicking receiver was like a death knell.
I walked upstairs and yelled to the sky,
'There is no God!'

Two weeks later… I am distraught.
Depressed.
I go to the doctors: he prescribes tranquillizers.

It's early morning.
I'm at work. The tranqs make me feel unreal,
Like I'm looking at everything from a reversed telescope.
I flush the pills down the loo.
The horrible textile machines are thrashing in the
background.
I phone her.
Her mam answers.
'She doesn't want to talk to you. She's got a new boyfriend.'
Really? Five years and already someone else.
Her mother puts the phone down.
Now I know it's really over.
The heat from the textile machines oppress.
I've got to try and focus on fixing florescent lights.
It would take two years of Zombiefication
Before the pain would *begin* to cease.

25-2-19

They try
Justify their
Immoral actions
By vilifying
The victim.

9-3-19

Governments
Like to use
Euphemisms
To conceal
Their dastardly
Deeds.

9-3-19

I didn't see
A tree
Till I was 33.

9-3-19

The autocrats,
The megalomaniacs,
Can't quell
The dissemination
Of information.

Those who've
Got nothing to lose
Don't have to
Lick your shoes.

9-3-19

If we just
Consumed
What we need
Instead
Of acquisitive
Greed.

9-3-19

I don't care
What country
You're from,
You're still
Carrying
A gun.

9-3-19

I was going upstairs
With my cup of tea,
But I'm glad I stayed:
I saw a magnificent magpie
Pluck a purple grape
From the garden
And flew to a chimney.

9-3-19

CONQUISTADORS

You came to our pristine land with smiles
And held out your grasping hands with friendship.
You traded our gold for your glass beads.
Before long you had colonized our land
And you coerced us into industrially mining our gold.
The work was grim and arduous but your insatiable lust
For the yellow metal made you cruel and relentless.
You tried to enforce your God upon us,
Insisting our God was barbaric and false,
And if we did what you said we would be rewarded in heaven.
You enslaved us and claimed to be superior.

But now we rebel, we grow weary of your presence.
Hold that greedy encroaching man down!
He has no respect for our culture or our sacred land.
Hold down that greedy callous man!
Force open his mouth.
Force open that mouth who would deny us our language.
Melt the gold.
Make the gold boiling hot and molten.
Here is the gold, the gold for which you so crave.
Pour the molten gold into his mouth,
Down into his stomach.
Let the hot bubbling gold blister his skin.
Here! How do you like our gold now?

9-3-19

It is impossible
To recognise others
Until you
Recognise yourself.

9-3-19

Good Friday walk in woods. Myriad bird chorus.
Stillness in leaves. I spontaneously turn to a more
Obscure path. The trees hem me in, an arboreal hug.
What's that silhouette? Is it a dog?
I cautiously move forward expecting to see its owner.
No… wait… a deer! Right in front of me,
A deer munching leaves from lower branches.
I creep forward… Oh why am I without camera?!
I've been coming in these woods all my life
And this is only the second time I've seen a deer.
I creep forward. The deer looks up. It has seen me.
I stop and we watch each other, still as statues.
A perfect picture of a deer! Oh to have my camera!
Wait! Two more deer, three in total. A male with antlers.
He sees me, alternates between preening and gazing at me.
I watch in privileged appreciation at the woodland deer.
Then, they dissolve into the foliage, furtive, silent, stealthy,
Vanish without trace…

19-4-19

PUNK SPIRIT

I was working a stultifying 9 to 5 in a council office,
Barely alive.
My boss was an authoritative personality:
The type abused as a child,
Subservient to anyone above him,
Abuses anyone below him.
From the age of 17 to 20 I took this patronizing shit:
Then I heard the Angelic Upstarts.
It precipitated my rebellion.
I began answering back.
To cut a long story short, I got the sack.
I began playing guitar in my bedroom.
I was crap, but I learnt several chords.
We were awful.
We practised in my friend's garage.
Miracle of miracle, we got gigs in local pubs.
We felt ostracized by society, marginalized, ignored by
mainstream,
But we didn't care,
That was the point.
We got women, loads, groupies, one night stands.
They liked our bad boy image:
The black leather jacket, ripped jeans, safety pins.
One groupie began hassling me.
She was pregnant.
I told her to fuck off.

Do you know what the crazy bitch did?
She left the aborted baby on my doorstep!
Even anarchists have to report somethings to the police.
Our daily diet of alcohol and marijuana wasn't enough:
We began snorting Billy, speed, amphetamine.
It complimented our frenzied playing, raw energy on stage.
We spoke our minds, no tactfulness or diplomacy.
Some dug out candidness, thought it amusing;
Some took exception and were offended:
We laughed in their face.
I moved onto heroine.
Heroine was my lover:
It became the most important thing in my life.
Jacked up, stoned out my box:
Out there… out there… out there… no where…
The sun hurt my eyes.
I was a lost boy.
I sold all my possessions for a hit.
My immunity broke.
My heart couldn't take it.
I lay on the tiled floor of an empty apartment
Undiscovered for three weeks before anyone realised.
Decomposed: swarming flies above a grinning skull,
Defiantly smirking to the end.

20-4-19

The following poem is loosely based on a medieval French legend circa 1147 AD when a troubadour, a skilled court poet, Jaufre Rudel, falls in love with the Countess of Tripoli. He is the first infatuation poet, disavowing the practicalities of relationships. He falls in love with a portrait of her without ever seeing her in the flesh and pines away at a distance. He does eventually get to meet her…

Marcel, a poet from Toulouse, France, believed highly in romance
Despite living a solitary life buried in books.
Despite being a renowned poet, his muse had deserted him.
He had lost his inspiration, the dreaded writer's block.
One morning he was idly flicking through Le Monde
Perfunctorily reading articles,
When one suddenly caught his eye.
It was written by a female African politician, Imanthi Arjana.
She was writing about corrupt officials in her country,
How cash crops were flattening forests,
How money did not trickle down to the grass roots.
Marcel read enraptured and hung on every word.
Here was a politician he could relate to.
Then, he saw the photograph of her: she was beautiful.
He became immutably entranced.
His muse had returned.
He wrote a cursory love poem about this African politician, Imanthi.
He waxed lyrical about her principles, her ethics,
How he so concurred with her views.
He eloquently described her physical appearance.

And, as with all inspired poets, he got somewhat carried away.
After a couple of drafts, the poem was eventually finished.
He completed the poem in a single sitting of mad flurry.
He was quite happy with the results, confident of his own ability.
Then, he had a crazy notion,
It would be a shame for Imanthi to never see his handy work,
So he sought her on Facebook and posted the poem to her.
Days went by without reply and his anxiety grew.
He wished he'd never bothered.
But then, one marvellous day, the African politician, Imanthi Arjana, replied.
She had read the poem with much interest.
She liked how he had analysed her policies in verse.
He had demonstrated complete comprehension of her reasoning.
She felt flattered at his descriptions of her appearance
But a little dubious regarding their accuracy.
Marcel was overjoyed:
He read in raptures her praise at his writing skills.
He could not contain himself and wrote another poem
Expressing his gratitude at her reply.
Over the next two years Marcel took great interest in African politics.
The poet and the politician conversed via the internet on a regular basis.
Then, one day, she invited him to visit her.
He jumped at the opportunity, as he had never left Europe before.
He was afraid of flying: the myth of Icarus played on his mind.

So he booked a ticket on an ocean liner.
The trip was long and arduous;
The oceans were tempestuous.
Marcel, who had a delicate constitution, fell violently ill.
By the time he reached African shores, his condition was critical.
He was rushed to the local hospital and his prognosis was bleak.
Imanthi heard about his plight and hurriedly took a taxi to the hospital.
The poet lay pale and feverous.
As she walked through the door he smiled at her radiant beauty.
Her heart churned as she moved closer and gently cradled him in her arms.
Her hot tears splashed on his ashen face.
Marcel's smile broadened and he whispered, 'I love you,'
As he contentedly passed away.

21-4-19

DREAMS OF ELEVATION

I'm on a bus: I quietly hurtle along a country road.
The bus effortlessly takes off, steep diagonal,
Like a silent rocket into the sky.
I feel no fear: I sedately gaze through the window.
Outside are futuristic buildings and glorious greenery.
There is no driver, no passengers, but me.
As I rise, rise, rise…
I find myself on Immingham docks,
The place where I worked as a marine electrician
In my teens and early twenties.
I'm in the boilershop: everything is pristine.
No one is there, divine emptiness.
I'm working a nightshift.
The giant workshop doors are wide open:
A glorious moon shines.
The regal night sky luminescent purple.
Along the quay magnificent buildings tower.
I want to bathe in the beautiful night.
I run towards the inviting workshop doors:
As I run I rise to the rafters,
Rise, rise, rise…

22-4-19

I have experienced the incredible privilege of many *sui generis* visions over the years compelling me to adopt hierophantic proclivities in order to facilitate exegesis: perambulating in the woods a bright white equilateral triangle manifested before me informing me of a cosmic numinous; when I was mugged by three men with a gun and nearly lost my eye a week later a kachina vividly appeared in a dream as we chanted on a mountain top augmenting my morale; one morning on the threshold of waking after years of struggle to finally complete my degree a red mandala hovered before my eyes indicating auguries of wholeness etcetera.

1-5-19

I have spent productive solitary hours
Musing amongst trees and flowers.
On the duplicitous I have earnestly cogitated,
Their undisclosed motives clearly stated.
If one is to survive in a world insidious,
Should we accept certain humans habitually perfidious?
To stand idly by and turn a blind eye
Makes some accomplices to most hideous crime.
I am an ardent advocate of inclusivity.
The excluded can lull into defeated passivity
Or rouse into resistance indignantly.
We must speak candidly discerning travesty.
Those who abuse power should not have longevity.

4-5-19

The people around me were loud,
Unpredictable, with fragile self-control.
I decided to spend three weeks
At a monastery with Benedictine monks
To spiritually replenish and acquire wisdom.
Time slows here... no rush, but peace, quiet and calm.
We silently walk past each other, unobtrusive,
No need for small talk, no urge for approval or acknowledgement,
As we patiently go about our daily tasks.
Brother Alex methodically mixes the egg yolk with coloured pigment,
Tempera is dexterously applied within iconographic outlines:
'Each brushstroke a prayer,' he intones.
I fascinatingly watch as days serenely pass
The picture is incrementally built,
Gold leaf carefully applied to refulgent shining wings.
Once the picture is complete,
It is placed at the altar
Where the pious monk blesses his art with holy water:
A stylised image in glorious colour of
Arch Angel Michael.
After three weeks I peacefully departed the monastery
With profound spiritual insight,
To accept the idiosyncrasies and flaws of fellow humans,
As they should accept mine.

6-5-19

I'm not a monarchist: indeed, I believe the institute to be anachronistic: but here is one of the most famous stories in English history I have dramatised and put to dialogue.

KING AND CAKES

Guthrum, the marauding Viking leader and his warriors carried out a surprise attack on Alfred, king of the West Saxons whilst he was celebrating Twelfth Night. Alfred was caught off guard and had to flee his stronghold. He rode his panting steed in the covert of the stormy night from the city he once ruled. His retinue, soaked to the bone, loyally followed him through pelting rain and crashing lightening, unsure where to go. The Vikings were everywhere, so Alfred decided to shed his retinue and noble habiliments and pose as a peasant to avoid detection. Over the moors the lone king resolutely rode as thunder rumbled in the night. Up ahead, as lightening violently flashed, a hovel was espied. Alfred was desperate for shelter, so rode up to the hovel. He dismounted his powerful steed and boldly banged upon the door rattling the hinges. It was early morning and the occupants were soundly asleep. King Alfred furiously banged again, not accustomed to being denied. Eventually, Denewulf the swineherd, stirred. The door slowly creaked open. Denewulf saw the bedraggled and soaked man before him and instantly frowned.

'What the devil is the meaning of waking me at such an early hour!' the swineherd angrily yelled at the king.

'How dare you talk to your monarch in such a fashion!' Alfred instinctively rejoined.

'Oh! Oh! A mad man!' Denewulf growled, about to slam the door shut.

'Wait! Wait! I can prove who I say I am,' Alfred, calmer, said.

'Go on then!' the swineherd impatiently snapped, not believing a single word.

Alfred, from his tunic pocket, produced a ring with royal insignia, the seal of the king.

'This, peasant, is my credentials. Now let me in. The rain is belting down and I am cold and wet.'

The swineherd peered at the ring in the half-light. It seemed authentic enough, though he did not possess the germane knowledge for verification. This man's bearing and manner certainly was of no commoner. Denewulf felt befuddled: let a possible mad man into his home; or deny a king entrance, which would mean eventual consequences.

'Come in. Come in,' Denewulf reluctantly mumbled.

The king stepped over the threshold and gazed all around. The floor was strewn with hay and in the corner was a sow sleeping with a litter of piglets nuzzled against the teats. The king groaned at such living conditions.

'Now, peasant, is there anyone else living in this pitiful hovel?'

'Only my wife,' Denewulf replied, still most perplexed.

'Please do not inform her of my identity. I did not intend to reveal it to you. I must remain incognito. I am evading capture from Guthrum, the Viking leader, until my troops can rally and retaliate. Now, where do I sleep?' Alfred imperiously asked. The swineherd, too tired to think, pointed to a bundle of hay in the corner, still incredulous that this was actually Alfred, king of the West Saxons. Alfred looked at the scruffy looking bundle of hay and grunted his displeasure.

'I am a king, not a pig. Kings do not sleep in hay. I will take your bed and you can sleep in there,' Alfred, with a look of disgust, proclaimed.

'My wife's asleep in my bed, unless you want to claim her as well,' Denewulf defiantly rejoined.

'I will not tolerate insolence!' Alfred rebuked, but then thought about the situation, realised these were no ordinary times and that he must adapt, so relented. Alfred disapprovingly stared at the hay, reluctantly laid upon it, and had a restless night full of worry about his predicament.

In the morning the swineherd's wife, Aflet, was first to rise. She was most annoyed to see a dishevelled figure sleeping in the corner of the room. Aflet furiously called her husband.

'Wolfie! Wolfie! Why have you permitted this woebegone tramp to sleep in our house?' Aflet inquired.

The noise woke king Alfred. 'Madam, what is all that caterwauling?'

'Caterwauling?! Caterwauling?! Get out this instance!' the swineherd's wife bellowed.

Denewulf, the swineherd appeared.

'I see you've met my friend, dear wife,' Denewulf said. He was accustomed to his wife's boisterousness.

'Friend? I have known you forty years and never met this wretch before,' Aflet replied.

'I met him at the market last week. I promised him temporary shelter, ' Denewulf replied.

'How long do you plan having him staying here?' Aflet asked.

'If I may be permitted to sojourn approximately week, it would be most advantageous,' Alfred, king of the West Saxons said, realising diplomacy was the best way to placate the curmudgeonly wife.

'"Most advantageous?" You don't talk like any tramp I've heard,' Aflet said.

'Oh, I've picked up a bit of language from eaves dropping,' the king unconvincingly explained.

There followed much argument, but eventually it was agreed the king could stay in Denewulf's and Aflet's humble abode for a week, but after that, he must be on his way. Aflet, the swineherd's wife, made Alfred, the king of the West Saxons, work for his lodgings.

'Now, I want you to keep an eye on those cakes and make sure they don't burn,' she demanded.

King Alfred did not like being ordered around by this cantankerous old woman, but, despite her temper, he had grown fond of her straight talking no nonsense approach to life, and, besides, she always made sure he was well fed. Moreover, he had to conceal his identity, and complying to her wishes was expedient. As he gazed into the fire he saw thatches burning on English homes set alight by the fierce Guthrum and his Viking marauders. Alfred began formulating strategies how to win back his kingdom. As he schemed, the cakes began to burn.

'What! I told you to keep an eye on those cakes! You silly daydreamer!' she scolded.

The king snapped from his reverie and profusely apologised to the old woman. He was pleased she had rebuked him. It made him realise daydreaming was not going to achieve anything. Devastating action was required. He cordially thanked the frowning old woman and kissed her on the nose.

'We'll have none of that!' she exclaimed, half amused at the audacity.

Alfred, king of the West Saxons, went on to recapture his kingdom. Once back on the throne, he proceeded to make the swineherd, Denewulf, a bishop, a most radical decision at the time, and an early example of upward mobility.

8-5-19

SPARROWHAWK

As I wait for the bus
I turn to see you sat on a low ledge.
I am alerted by your alertness,
Hook-billed laser eyed sentinel.
You fluff scruffy feathers
To shield you from cold rain.
As you stare with huge yellow lamps
Into my mesmerized eyes
You defiantly shit before me,
Urban predator,
Autonomous sky-dweller,
Anarchic acrobat,
Carnivorous opportunist.
You rip paper sparrows to shreds
With scalpel beak precision
Discarding forlorn feathers in a bloody pile.
I love those little tweeties
But you must live too.
Then, with fanned feathered grace
You effortlessly ascend to roof.
My bus arrives
As I take one last look
At magnificent aplomb.

11-5-19

A four year apprenticeship from leaving school
Then two years fully qualified: marine electrician.
Docker, up at 6.30am in the ice.
Cold siren wails, everybody in.
Large resolute ships all dry-docked,
Brass propellers grasping winter air.
Beefy boiler makers spitting beer.
No time for the weak here.
Hazards galore.
My hand trapped on lowering gang plank
Could have flattened my hand flat,
Just before full weight settled
Forcefully pulled it out as swearing spat.
Busbars look innocuous, dead,
But throbbing energy will kill your touch:
You gotta be careful, cautious,
Always double check.
Loud staccato sound of riveters
Will damage ear drums.
Hiss of the burners cutting deck head,
You will be cut in half by falling plate.
Lost a finger, my mate.
Another testicles squashed by falling weight.
'Heigh ho!' 'Salubrious!' are the calls of graft.
Each a master of his craft.
Union meetings for any dispute.
Men will not remain mute.
No hesitation of strike if demands not met:
It was a death knell when Humber Ship Repairers finally closed.
The yard eerily empty and quiet now.
Dry docks permanently water-filled.
Sound of work permanently killed.

11-5-19

Last night I was watching the movie *Rumble Fish* as recommended to me by one of my students. (By the by, rumble fish are fish that fight each other in a tank but when free in a river leave each other alone. The frustrations of confinement are apparent.) One of the main characters, Motorcycle Boy, played subtly by Mickey Rourke, was fascinated by these fish, gazing at them for hours in the pet shop. The fish had been isolated in separate compartments, and Motorcycle Boy pitied their solitary existence: maybe he associated their remoteness with his own. You could never tell if Motorcycle Boy was crazy or not, such was the understatement of the script and acting. For an ex-gang leader he was most learned. He mentions Greek mythology, Cassandra: she was loved by Apollo and hence gave her the gift of prophecy, but when she spurned him, he cursed her to always feel compelled to prophecy the truth but with no one ever believing her. Motorcycle Boy later talks about how indigenous tribes venerate the lunatic because they believe he/she has divine insight: I had read similar in books on psychoanalysis.

I knew a man who was rejected by society so he lived in seclusion and retreated into the recesses of his mind. There, in sustained introspection, he inadvertently discovered in his psyche the archetypes, ancient symbols common to all cultures. At first, he did not know what they meant, but after years of rumination, he discovered their significance. From esoteric cogitation he was able to transcend, elevate, individuate. I met this man one day. He earnestly asseverated: 'When I look at people I see them clearly; but when they look at me they do not see who I am.' 'Really?' I replied, 'you see them but they don't see you?' He nodded and smiled. 'How could they know?' he said. 'How do I achieve such acute perception?' I asked. 'Regularly hold a mirror up to yourself, not narcissistically, but honestly and critically.' 'Is that all?' I said. 'It's not as easy as you think,' he replied.

13-5-19

A book
Is a mirror
In which you
Discover
Yourself.

22-5-19

If spring never came winter would always be here.
Cloudy skies instead of clear.
I would pine for leaves on trees.
Miss the gentle hum of bees.
Wild flowers would only live in my head.
Mother nature forever dead?
No, she would eventually raise her head.
Clemency invites blue welcome skies.
Humming of bees awakening trees.
Red admiral with smiling wings.
Blackbird happily sings.
Sit outside with cup of tea.
Suburbia with a hint of rurality.
Ants forage on the ground.
I feed them kipper scraps.
Sparrows drink from watering can.
When I'm still their confident grows.
Love to hear feathered beating wings.
Rapid pulse as they take flight.
A murmuration of starlings swiftly descend
And ravenously eat crumbs of bread.
Sights of spring sing in my head.

22-5-1

TOM

Look, when she moved into the room next door, I was intending to be a gentleman. I actually couldn't believe my luck. She was gorgeous, I mean, film star material. What she was doing moving into this pokey little bedsit I just don't know. She could have been on the cover of Vogue. She could have easily made wads of cash from her looks. Much to my disappointment, I actually didn't see her that much. Occasionally, I could hear her music playing. One evening, after mooching around town all day, I was walking past her window on the way to the front door. Her curtains were slightly open and a chink of light shone through. Keep walking Tom… No… Wait… Take a look through the gap. You know you want to. What if she sees me? She won't see you. Take a look. Go on. Well, nosiness got the better of me. So I took a look. What did I see? I couldn't believe my luck. She was actually undressing. That was it. I couldn't take my eyes away. She slipped her blouse off. Her body! I was mesmerized. She was about to unclip her bra when she looked directly at me. Yipes! She saw me. My heart sank. She stormed over to the window as she put her dressing gown on. 'What do you think you're doing?!' she yelled. 'Er, er, I dunno,' I feebly said. 'You peeping Tom!' she shouted and angrily closed the curtains. It wasn't long after that she moved out. My excuse, she was gorgeous. I couldn't resist. I know, I know, curiosity killed the cat. My voyeurism killed any possibility of friendship.

22-5-19

The grass, alas, is screaming.
It had been gently growing,
But now the mower is mowing.
The daisies are crazy with despair:
We can no longer put them in our hair.

22-5-19

Let the human race develop in glorious diversity.
Let language reveal the spirit of the speaker.
Let our judgements be made on rigorous reason.
Within our dialectical disputes we can find truth.
Are your explanations satisfactory?
Do numeracy and geometry have spiritual significance?
Absorb environment with equanimity.
Adaptation facilitates survival.
The deep structures of your mind are of the universal kind.
Cohesive society, not dichotomy.
Sensuality and spirituality essential.
If they derogate your flow, grow…
No one can thwart your thoughts,
Exploratory internal discourse.
Channel emotion into productivity.
Unsullied love ensures the well-being of others.
Do not be seduced by the darkness.
Like a sunflower, turn towards the light.

22-5-19

People proliferate at alarming rate.
Villages grow into towns grow into cities.
Conurbations surge and merge.
Trees are razed for a train.
Deer is road kill by the curb.
Fox's domain begins to wane.
Sparrows live in garden hedge.
Squirrel buries nuts on the lawn.
Turtle throttled by plastic noose.
Atmosphere saturated with fossil fuel.
Earth's resources rapidly drained.
Environmental pressure groups petitioned for years.
Politicians only just beginning to wake.
I only hope it's not too late.

22-5-19

Hi. Pleased to meet you. Did you know you could die and be unaware of it? You may wonder who I am. I'll introduce myself at the end. Well, well, the day has come at last, the momentous day. The day written in all religions. You see, I've been watching you, all of you, closely, very closely, nothing more intimate. In fact, from the day you were born I've been observing you. I've watched every moment of your life, your pains, your joys, everything. And yes, I've known every thought you've ever had. What thoughts! How imaginative! But don't worry, all humans are duplicitous, two-faced. You've got to be to survive in society. I mean, if everyone spoke their mind all the time, what discord there would be. You need a significant portion of circumspection for a cohesive society. Those who always speak their minds are labelled eccentrics and become outcasts. Are you the person you wanted to be? Is your ideal self at odds with who you really are? Don't worry, most have cognitive dissonance. So, what is today, the momentous day I speak of? It *is* the most important day of your existence. It is, wait for it, your judgement day! Yep, the day when you have to justify yourself to me. Oh, the excuses I've heard, you won't believe. But no one can escape judgement. Every detail of your life has been recorded. I will be playing back to you key moments of your life. I know, you have regrets, you've changed, you've made amends. Who am I? Well the ancient Egyptians know me as Anubis, the dude with the weighing scales; the ancient Greeks knew me as Radamanthus, the judge of the dead; the Hindus know me as Yama, the god of death. Whatever, you can call me The Grand Inquisitor. So, your judgement day is here. Here it is. Now, justify yourself.

24-5-19

RELATIONSHIP
HISTORY FAILURE

Sweet Karen, I saw her across the buzzing classroom.
She was blessed with vivacious beauty.
I could not avert my gaze.
When she showed interest in me I was truly amazed.
I was overwhelmed with emotion,
Felt unworthy and reduced to inarticulate nonsense.
She slipped through my fingers, this shining star.
I continued to admire her from afar.

Volatile Trix, stayed for five years, became my fiancé.
She reluctantly tolerated my immature nature.
She was gorgeous, won a lovely legs competition.
I encouraged her to wear stockings to show them pins.
The only reciprocating loving relationship I was ever in.
She wanted to have my baby: I wanted to drink, fuck other
women and be crazy.
When she left me I knew only despair.
It took years to get her out of my hair.

Divine Chloe, art teacher, on first seeing knew she was special.
I became mesmerized with her profound philosophical mind.
She introduced me to feminism in art.
I would have given her my heart.
We went for coffee but I was erratically stoned.
When art history finished I was again alone.
But the seeds of female equality in my mind were sown.

Mystical Maria, Greek girl, English Literature undergraduate, ocean eyes.
I was drowning in her smile.
She spoke my name like music.
We would listen to The Beatles and get monumentally stoned.
I would have made Greece my home.
But one time, wrecked, I became paranoid about my hair.
That, unfortunately, was the end of her.

Exotic Rupa, Indian girl, psychology student,
So beautiful, so unassuming, so smart.
After two years she had stolen my heart.
Our weekends in London remain a treasured memory.
There was no intimacy, though I remember her affectionately touching my hand
Before entering an art gallery.
She was the first time conversations were sustained and meaningful.
But her father didn't approve of white boy.
She knew my yearning and grew quite coy.
She couldn't give me what I desired.
She let me go that new year's eve night.
How desolate I felt at our last goodbye.

The wonderful girls I knew whilst emotionally immature.
Too easily moved, impetuously falling in love.
Doomed to failure like Romeo and Juliet.
The Friar advised Romeo: *'Wisely and slow;*
They stumble that run fast.'
That was the brief story of each favourite lass.

6-6-19

All the stars
In the sky
Could not
Fill her eyes.

11-6-19

More people
Have been killed
For speaking the truth
Than for speaking lies.

11-6-19

From
A
Fist
To
A
Flower.

11-6-19

At the weekend I watched the excellent movie Peterloo. I first became aware of the incident through the Percy Bysshe Shelley poem. In 1815 the workers of Manchester and Lancashire had many grievances with government: under paid; poor working conditions; unfair Corn Laws; and no one to represent them in parliament. A mass meeting of the workers was organized at Peter's Field in Manchester. The meeting was peaceful, the people unarmed, and women and children were among them. The government incited the riot act and ordered the Yeoman Guard, who killed 10-20 innocent civilians and injured up to 700. During the movie it was demonstrated how unfair the judicial system was. My poem encapsulates one of the cases. A destitute worker steals a coat from his boss and sentenced to death.

He has two coats.
I have none.
I always feel cold
At the setting sun.
He has two coats.
I stole one.
Now he has one coat.
I have one.
And now I'm going
To be hung.

11-6-19

PERSPICACITY

As I was sat at the bus stop a man walked past chuntering to himself. He seemed to be arguing and took on the role of two different personas. Well, I know I sometimes talk to myself in private: but this man was in an intense dialogue with himself in full view of the public. I have worked in mental health so his behaviour did not unsettle me.

The bus pulled up and I nonchalantly stepped on. As I paid for my ticket I scanned around for an empty seat. The bus was quite full: but amongst the hustle and bustle of the passengers, in stark contrast to the surrounding chattering, sat a man most still with eyes blazing. I felt quite uneasy for he had noticed me noticing him. His facial expression never altered, unemotional, almost vacant, but so alert. Oh, he looked human enough, if it wasn't for his preternatural calmness and piercing peculiar eyes. I hastily found myself a seat. I would have preferred sitting behind him so I could monitor him, but there was only a seat in front. As the bus pulled away I could feel his eyes burning in the back of my head. I felt vulnerable and powerless. An alien, a being from another planet, sat on my local bus, and none of the other passengers suspected a thing as they chattered away. As each stop passed I ardently hoped he would egress. Then I had an alarming thought: what if he waited until I exited and followed me home. I shuffled uncomfortably in my seat. My stop was approaching and I thought of staying on the bus until he departed. What if he was waiting for me to make a move? The passengers idly chatted oblivious to the extra-terrestrial amongst them. Was this the beginning of an invasion force, first observing our behaviour to assess our weaknesses? My stop approached and I threw caution to the wind, dinged the bell (which sounded like a death knell), and I nervously stood up to egress. Shock! The extra-terrestrial stood up too. I stared at him in wide eyed horror. His bulbous head scraped the ceiling and his intense eyes pierced my fear.

I jumped from the bus, not thanking the driver as accustomed. Staring straight ahead, I quickly strode down the street. What should I do? Walk home? Lead him to where I live? My head was dazed and confused. I couldn't aimlessly roam around the streets indefinitely. I decided to head for the safety of my home. Safety?! He probably had the technology to easily enter a locked door.

I stepped through my gate, fumbled my keys out of my pocket, struggled to locate the key in the lock, hastily unlocked the front door, quickly stepped in and slammed the door shut. Maybe he would walk on by. Maybe he was gone. I nervously peered through the window. I couldn't see him. But suddenly his huge bulk stood before the window. His eyes were now nothing like human, but large and black shining like a tarantula's, staring into my room. I yelped and made for the phone. I heavily poked 999 and asked for the police.

'Yes?'

'There's an extra-terrestrial staring through my window.'

'Calm down. There's a what?'

'I noticed him on the bus.'

'Noticed whom?'

'He's followed me home.'

'Who has?'

'An alien from another planet.'

'Is this some kind of joke?'

'No! No! They've invaded! They're amongst us!' I yelled. The police hung up.

'Help! Help!' I blurted down the phone, but to no avail.

I stalked around the room, frantic. What should I do? In my panic I decided to confront him. I opened my front door. There he was, neck pulsing and reptilian lips quivering, clouds reflected in his large black shining eyes, eight orbs gazing at me.

'What do you want?' I manically inquired.

'You know my identity,' he calmly replied.

'I know nothing,' I pleaded.

'You know,' he confirmed.

'I won't say a thing,' I promised.

'You've just phoned the police, but they didn't believe you. We can't have our identity revealed. I must eliminate you.'

He slowly put his hand in his pocket. I believed he was reaching for a ray gun or something. I fell to my knees begging for mercy.

'Please! Please! I'll do anything you say!' I whimpered.

That's how my neighbours saw me. They were concerned at my unusual behaviour, how I was so distressed, jabbering something about aliens. And that's why you've sectioned me in this psychiatric ward, doctor. I tried to persuade you and other psychoanalysts and the nurses that aliens were living amongst us, shoulder to shoulder, completely undetected, that earth is in imminent danger from beings from another planet, why, doctor, you may be an extra-terrestrial for all I know. It was my mistake to see through one's disguise. Why are you shaking your head in disapproval doctor? I'm not crazy! They're here! They're here! Don't just sit there and do nothing. Inform the military!

With that, a nurse produced a huge syringe. I am pumped with enough sedative to comatose an elephant...

13-6-19

Where
Her tears
On the ground
Splash,
Flowers grow
In a
Flash.

25-6-19

ON LISTENING TO AURORA'S: A DIFFERENT KIND OF HUMAN.

We've been watching you, gentle heart.
We watch your internal struggle,
How goodness is prevailing,
How you spread love,
How you care for those in distress,
How you are concerned for the future of your planet.
You are not alone, gentle heart, strong heart.
There are many like you, waiting.
They know about you, precious one.
They are impressed with your endeavours.
They think your world is too harsh for you.
We want you to go with us to our world, across the galaxy.
You'd love it there: our world is at peace, unpolluted.
No one lives in fear. What do you think?
Consider our offer. It would be truly home.

25-6-19

I have Viking blood.
I have a Scandinavian name.
Teach me about Norway
Musician who will not be tamed.

Teach me about Norway
Beautiful girl.
My ancestors are from there
Though travelled the world.

I hear it's picturesque
With many fjords.
Teach me about Norway,
I wouldn't get bored.

Teach me about Norway
'Cause part of me is there.
One day I hope to breathe
The crisp Nordic air.

25-6-19

On reading Wordsworth.

It is midnight.
The woods are still and dark.
Black clouds fill the sky.
A gentle zephyr coaxes the clouds
To sail on by.
The moon is gradually revealed,
Full, and gloriously shining.
This awakens the nightingale's song.
The nightingale gleefully sings
At the unveiling of the moon.

5-7-19

Bongo boy sojourns in lush fields on outskirt of town.
Rhythmically plays his bongos as radiant sun goes down.
As irresistible tribal beat facilitates transcendence
Soul cultivates attachment to solar energy.
Oh child of the cosmos with heterodox spirituality
The orange sun sitting on the horizon bids you farewell.
Moon appears, refulgent silver light, as bongo beat
Initiates metempsychosis, permeating into lunar light.
Bongo boy dilates into the star encrusted night.

29-7-19

THE REVENANT

The churchyard is illuminated by a bright full moon.
The soil is deep, dark and damp.
I lay in the frozen ground like a fetus
Though dead and decomposing.
Bloodless grey skin with deep lacerations.
My mind longs to see the sky.
My elbow grinds as I stretch my arm upwards
And break the surface of the hallowed ground.
My rigor mortis hand tries to grasp the louring clouds.
From my arid mouth pours forth a guttural anguished cry.
I yearn to extricate from this shallow grave.
Instinct summons me upwards from the fetid mound.
I drag my unresponsive feet across the moonlit churchyard,
The shadow of a woman on my vacant brain.
I must find the girl that haunts my heart.
Unyielding love compels me to live again.

29-7-19

Don't deny the sadness, let it flow,
That way you can let it go.

The human body is so frail:
I shiver in the snow and hail.

I have plumbed the depths of despair,
That's why I'm laughing flying in the air.

The moth flies in the night
Yearning for the light.

Those most aware they're going to die
Are those who feel most alive.

30-7-19

On hearing an Aurora interview where she said school often bored her and she invented a story to convince her friends talking mice were going to take over the school.

Sciences are crucial for furthering our knowledge and raising people's well-being, and I actually take an interest in the sciences, but for the sake of this story…

There was this beautiful and clever girl, but despite being clever she found school dreadfully boring. She sat in math's class listening about equations and shuffled restlessly in her seat. 'How boring,' she sighed. She sat in physics listening about gravity and stared through the window in a daydream. 'How boring,' she sighed. She sat in biology listening about internal organs and impatiently drummed her fingers on the desk, and, yes, you guessed it, she sighed, 'How boring.'

As days passed this beautiful and clever girl got more bored. She got so bored that during one math's lesson she began to tell her friends that the school was going to be taken over by mice, but these were no ordinary mice, they were speaking mice. At first her friends didn't believe her story, but daily she persisted in this story determined to convince them. She didn't believe the story herself, she told it because she was bored. 'The school is going to be taken over by talking mice,' she would say. Until, one day, such was her eloquence, she convinced all her friends that talking mice would take over the school.

Days passed, but no talking mice appeared. Her friends then began to disbelieve her. 'You silly thing,' they would say, 'telling fibs like that.'

But one morning, as the children walked into math's, the math's teacher was not sat there, but a mouse! The children were most surprised to see the mouse sat there, but they became even more surprised when the mouse said, 'Today we are not going to do math's, but learn some songs.' And so all through the lesson the mouse taught the children songs. The children had great fun all singing together. It was then time to go to the physics lesson. But as the children walked in the classroom the physics teacher was not sat there, but a mouse! The mouse said, 'Today we are not going to do physics, but learn how to play piano.' And so all through the lesson the children learnt chords. They were not very good at first, but by the end of the lesson, some actually got the hang of it. The time came for the biology lesson, and as the children walked into the classroom, they saw their usual teacher was not sat there, but a mouse! The mouse said, 'Today we are not going to do biology, but learn to paint pictures.' And so all lesson the children painted wonderful pictures of trees, animals, and the beautiful and clever girl painted a glorious moth. Her prophecy had come true.

The school was now being run by speaking mice. The little girl was never bored at school again.

10-8-19

The morning sky was bluer than blue.
I plunged into its infinite depth.
The sun cascaded golden showers.
Scientists may clinically say
The sun works by nuclear fusion:
But I say the sun is a miracle,
Precipitator of heterogeneous life.
The lawn was greener than green:
I walked barefoot to feel
The cool blades between my toes.
The sparrows peck bread and sip water,
Little fellows look at me quizzically
As I smile at their bright eyes.
I have literally had a revolver at my head.
My smile says life is a blessed privilege.

14-8-19

I conjecture on the execution dream that contributed in changing Stephen Hawkin's attitude.

I was at Oxford University, not really applying myself,
A casual approach, 1 hour study a day.
I was doing just enough to pass assignments.
Procrastination was my forte.

As I laid in my dorm one sunny afternoon
Rehearsing my patter for coxswain
(I had developed a reputation for steering
Oxford's rowing boats and effectively cajoling the crew)
I fell into deep slumber...

I sat in a gloomy prison cell.
They were roughly shaving my head.
The cold blade scraped over my scalp, nicking my skin.
Then they shaved my calf, pulling at my hairs.
'What are you doing?' I muttered, utterly bewildered.
'That's to improve conductivity,' one matter-of-factly said.
A clergyman drifted in and began issuing prayers in Latin.
He then asked me, 'Do you have any last words?'
'Last words?! What's happening? Where am I?'
With that, two burly prison officers grabbed hold of my arms
And ushered me down a poorly lit corridor.
On either side were prisoners peering through iron bars
Clattering their metal drinking mugs.
One said, 'Goodbye amigo!'
My legs and arms were shackled by iron chains
And they clunked with every step I took.
A dark sense of foreboding pervaded me as I shuffled along.

We entered an austere chamber, and there before me
Was a menacing wooden chair with leather straps.
My skin crawled with fear.
'Wait! Wait! This is a mistake!
What am I supposed to have done?!' I manically yelled.
No one said a word.
The silence was heavy and oppressive.
They unceremoniously pushed me into the chair
And fastened down my wrists, waist and ankles.
I put up a token struggle but knew it was futile to resist.
I looked around the death chamber:
In front of me was a solemn audience with dark eyes peering.
They then fastened electrodes to my head and leg
Along with wet sponges:
The cold water on my sensitive skin made me recoil in panic.
I tried pulling at the straps but they held me down firm.
I gazed around the room in mute horror
Trying to appeal for sympathy:
But they all sat still, apparently indifferent.
I could not recall any of my previous life,
The heinous crime I had committed to deserve such
'A cruel and unusual punishment'.
Then a lever was thrown.
It made the chamber lights dim.
My muscles began to violently convulse.
My face grotesquely contorted.
I lost control of my bowels and unwittingly defecated.
An acrid smell of frying bacon imbued the room.

One of my eyeballs began to melt.
Flames burst from my head.
For 15 minutes 2450 volts
Cruelly surged through my frail writhing body.
Finally, I had cardiac arrest…

I insouciantly floated above the electric chair.
It suddenly occurred to me that I maybe having a nightmare,
So I ardently forced myself awake.
As I mercifully extricated from slumber I heard an earnest
voice cry:
'Live life with purpose!'

My eyes suddenly opened
And I found myself in my familiar bed
In the Oxford dorm.
I yelled out in profound relief.
I jumped out of bed with alacrity, had a hearty breakfast, then
eagerly dived into study.
All day I had my head buried in wonderful books.
From that moment on I diligently applied myself.
I eventually became a distinguished professor.
I greatly advanced quantum mechanics.
Indeed, I became a world renowned theoretical physicist,
Some say a global icon.

Time is the most valuable commodity we possess:
Do not waste it!

1-9-19